THE AMERICAN COLONIZATION SOCIETY AND THE CREATION OF THE LIBERIAN STATE

THE AMERICAN COLONIZATION SOCIETY AND THE CREATION OF THE LIBERIAN STATE

A Historical Perspective, 1822-1900

Amos J. Beyan, Ph.D.
Youngstown State University
Youngstown, Ohio

UNIVERSITY
PRESS OF
AMERICA

Lanham • New York • London

University Press of America®, Inc.
4720 Boston Way
Lanham, Maryland 20706

3 Henrietta Street
London WC2E 8LU England

Printed in the United States of America
British Cataloging in Publication Information Available

Library of Congress Cataloging-in-Publication Data

Beyan, Amos Jones.
The American Colonization Society and the creation of the Liberian state : a historical perspective, 1822-1900 / Amos J. Beyan.
p. cm.
Includes bibliographical references and index.
1. Liberia—Politics and government—To 1944.
2. American Colonization Society. I. Title.
DT633.B49 1990 966.62—dc20 90–46426 CIP

ISBN 0–8191–7991–4 (cloth : alk. paper)
ISBN 0–8191–7992–2 (pbk. : alk. paper)

The paper used in this publication meets the minimum requirements of American National Standard for Information Sciences—Permanence of Paper for Printed Library Materials, ANSI Z39.48–1984.

ACKNOWLEDGMENTS

This study would not have been completed had it not been for the support and guardianship I received from friends, the University of Liberia, West Virginia University, scholars on the topic, my parents, and family.

I would, therefore, like to extend my sincere thanks to Mr. and Mrs. Stephen J. Kelly of Clinton, New York, for their extensive financial aid and moral support throughout the preparation of the study. Actually I owe them a lot more than can be expressed here. This appreciation is also extended to West Virginia University which offered me financial assistance during the research for the study, and to the University of Liberia which awarded me, through its former key administrators, Dr. Mary A. B. Sherman, Dr. Pal Chaudhuri, Dr. Patrick L. N. Seyon, Dr. J. Teah Tarpeh, and Dr. Amos Sawyer, a faculty research grant.

Appreciation is extended to Dr. Robert G. Gregory of Syracuse University whose advice and personal encouragement reinforced my interest in African History. I also thank Dr. K. C. Morrison and Dr. Otey Scruggs, both of Syracuse University, and the late Dr. Nathan Huggins, formerly of Columbia University, for introducing me to African-American History.

I must also express my sincere gratitude to Dr. Rodger Yeager, Dr. William Mcleod, Dr. Jack Hammersmith, and the late Dr. Carl Hunt for reading the early draft of the study. A special acknowledgment is extended to Dr. Robert Maxon for his many useful criticisms and suggestions. This acknowledgment is also rendered to Mrs. Mary T. Belloto of Youngstown State University for typing and proofreading the work, to Dr. Martin Berger for proofreading the final draft, and to the Youngstown State University Graduate School that offered me a faculty research grant that helped with the cost of the work.

I am indebted to my late parents Mamai and Kolubah for their sacrifices which paved the way to my receiving a western education. Finally, my thanks are extended to my wife, Phyllis, and sons, Kolubah and Stephen Quoi-Quoi, whose collective assistance and love made the completion of the study possible.

TABLE OF CONTENTS

MAPS

INTRODUCTION

This is a study of nineteenth century Liberia. Unlike most previous studies of the history of that West African nation, it provides neither a detailed narrative of the colonization movement in the United States nor a full account of the organization it spawned, the American Colonization Society (ACS). Both these aspects have been treated in varying amounts of detail by numerous scholars. Rather, this study explains, by a selective analysis drawing on historical examples, the development of political, economic, and religious institutions of Liberia. It argues that these were largely extensions of the institutional values inherent in the ACS and the economic and social forces at work on the coastal region that became Liberia in the nineteenth century.

This examination of Liberian history draws heavily on the wealth of material written on the ACS. The first serious work on the ACS was written by John McPherson in 1891, and the second by Early Fox in 1919. These were followed by many other scholarly works which, unfortunately, have emphasized the American aspect of the ACS, almost completely ignoring the Liberian phase.[1] The ACS and its mission inspired a number of important published works in the nineteenth and early twentieth century. These may be conveniently divided into those that were written to glorify the motives and activities of the ACS,[2] and those which condemn the objectives and practices of that organization.[3] The significance of these works is that their opposing themes illustrate the contradictions which were inherent in the ACS. Tom W. Shick's book is unlike all these works. In his study of the development of social and political institutions in Liberia, Shick views them, especially the former, as fundamentally an initiative of the Afro-Americans who were sent to what became Liberia.[4] The present study, on the other hand, views the ACS as the main source of Liberia's institutions and values.

The net impact of the ACS on Liberia cannot be thoroughly understood without first examining the organization. The values and beliefs which characterized the prominent supporters of the ACS must be taken into consideration. This description includes identifying prominent members of the ACS, and their social backgrounds, values, religious beliefs, and political and economic concepts (associated with the dominant slaveowning class of the Old South) since the effects of these backgrounds and attitudes on the ACS and the colony it founded were enormous. This explains why the first chapter of the study is addressed to the social backgrounds of the leading members of the ACS.

But it would be misleading to maintain that the ACS was the only social determinant of the Liberian entity. There were other forces at work which helped to shape the historical development of Liberia. An important process, still only partially understood by historians, was the evolution of the political and social formations of the region which became Liberia in the nineteenth century. Chapter II draws on the sparse and often contradictory sources to provide a brief description of the ethnic groups resident there.[5] It also provides an account of the commercial advances of the Europeans on the coast of West Africa and the Africans' response to the advances before the 1820s. These created innovative trends, such as new commercial activity, social stratification, and the emergence of a non-traditional coastal elites.

As treated in Chapters II and III, these ongoing social processes were to serve as barriers to the ACS' colonization effort. The obstruction was a direct consequence of the fear the new coastal elites and their African counterparts held that the advance of the ACS on the coast of pre-Liberia posed a serious threat to their new social status. This consternation was further reinforced by the fact that the ACS' colonization initiative was also associated with the attempt to stop the transatlantic slave trade, a trade that sustained the social status of the new coastal elites. As implied in Chapter III the opposition to the ACS' advance, nevertheless, created social conditions that only reinforced the dependence of the Liberian settlers on the ACS.

The dependent relationship that existed between the settlers and the ACS was intensified by the commercial progress of the various European powers on the coast of pre-colonial, colonial, and independent Liberia. As examined in Chapters IV and V, the intensified commercial advance of the Europeans came to threaten colonial and later independent Liberia. Unable to arrest this trend, the settlers concluded that they would not survive politically without wholeheartedly accepting the social culture of paternalism and other institutional values that had already been introduced in Liberia by the ACS. This explains why most of the settlers, during the colonial and early independent period, accepted the social arrangements introduced by the ACS without much protest.

Independent Liberia's emerging leadership ensured the development of this inclination through its invocation of Liberian nationalism. While the emphasis on nationalistic sentiment assisted in bringing the settlers together against the increasing commercial advance of the Europeans, it also, at the time, helped to mitigate the diverse internal oppositions to the social domination of those rulers. It is, therefore, argued that the neutralization of such opposition was a triumph of the leaders of independent Liberia since it helped them to assert and maintain their political and social supremacy. This, of course, meant the continuation of the institutional values introduced by the ACS which included its patriarchal and paternalistic social arrangements.

It is further emphasized in Chapter V that the world economic system, represented by the commercial activities of the various European merchants on the coast of pre-colonial, colonial, and independent Liberia, was among the main reinforcers of the institutional values introduced in Liberia by the ACS. Its impact in shaping Liberia's economic development was clearly illustrated as that country grew. The dependent relationship which existed between the ACS and Liberia was increasingly modified by the world mode of production to meet its needs. In the process, the economic interests of the Liberian merchants, who were also the political and social leaders of their country, were subordinated to those of their European counterparts. In other words, the merchants of Liberia increasingly became dependent on the European merchants. Before the end of the period under consideration, Liberian merchants, who had earlier dominated the commerce of their country, were, in fact, reduced to petty traders, serving the interests of European commercial firms.

Despite the fact that the world economic system placed the Liberian merchants on a lower rung of the economic order, this did not necessarily mean that it destroyed them. On the contrary, it continued to enhance their social domination in Liberia. This was made possible because the minimal material gain they procured from their ancillary involvement with the world economic system was invested so as to insure their social supremacy. No wonder the foregoing social group continued to monopolize nearly all the most important social and political institutions throughout the period covered by this study.

It is demonstrated in Chapter V that the above development was very similar to the social arrangements that had been introduced in Liberia by the ACS. This seems to explain why they continued to assist each other's development, though the process was not always amicable.

The final chapter contends that the different western churches established in Liberia were among the reinforcers of that country's institutional developments. The religious doctrines and values emphasized by these churches were, for example, similar to the religious emphasis of the ACS that not only was Liberia God's creation but also that the deeds of the country were divinely foreordained. Although this helped to ensure the social hegemony of the Liberian rulers, such a religious emphasis tended to discourage critical treatment of Liberia's secular problems since the shortcomings of that nation could easily be attributed to providence. It is not surprising that even their view of a civilized person or society was defined in a Christian context and the worldly values emphasized by that religion.

The social arrangements described so far were not without opposition. From its inception up to the present century, Liberia has always been vulnerable to social violence. The first major incident took place in 1823, the second in 1871, and the third in 1980. These violent social disruptions were largely the direct consequence of the failure of the social arrangements noted above to accommodate economically and politically large numbers of the Liberian populace. It may, therefore, be inferred that unless Liberia radically modifies the legacy it inherited from the ACS, it will remain a victim of underdevelopment and, of course, the social turbulence that is usually generated by it.

NOTES

Introduction

[1]The following works emphasize the American origin and organization of the ACS, but they almost completely ignore the Liberian aspect: Frederic Bancroft, "The Colonization of American Negroes, 1816-1865," in Jacob E. Cook, ed., *Frederic Bancroft, Historian* (Norman, 1957), pp. 147-191; Charles I. Foster, "The Colonization of Free Negroes in Liberia, 1816-1835," *Journal of Negro History*, XXXVIII (1953); Early L. Fox, *The American Colonization Society, 1816-1840* (Baltimore, 1919); Kent P. Opper, "The Minds of White Participants in the African Colonization Movement, 1816-1840," (Ph.D. Dissertation, University, of North Carolina, 1972); Eli Seifman, "A History of the New York Colonization Society," (Ph.D. Dissertation, New York University, 1965); Henry N. Sherwood, "The Formation of the American Colonization Society," *Journal of Negro History* II (1917); Phil Sigler, "The Attitude of Free Blacks Toward Emigration to Liberia, "(Ph.D. Dissertation, Boston University, 1969); Philip Staudenraus, *The African Colonization Movement, 1816-1865* (New York, 1961); Charles H. Wesley, "Lincoln's Plan for Colonization of the Emancipated Slaves," *Journal of Negro History*, IV (1919); Werner Wickstron, "The American Colonization Society and Liberia: An Historical Study in Religious Motivation and Achievement," (Ph.D. Dissertation, Hartford Seminary, 1949).

[2]This group includes such works as: Archibald Alexander, *A History of Colonization on the West Coast of Africa*, (Philadelphia, 1846); Fox, *The American Colonization Society*; Frederick Freeman, *Yaradee: A plea for Africa in Familiar Conversations on the Subject of Slavery and Colonization* (Philadelphia, 1836); Ralph R. Gurley, *Life of Jehudi Ashmun, Late Colonial Agent in Liberia* (Washington, 1835); *Mission to England on Behalf of the American Colonization Society* (Washington, 1836); Thomas Hodkins, *An Inquiry into the Merits of the American Colonization Society and a Reply*

to the Charge Brought Against it with an Account of the British African Colonization Society (London, 1833).

[3]This group includes such works as: Samuel Cornish and Theodore S. Wright, *The Colonization Scheme Considered in its Reflection by the Colored People* (Newark, 1840); William L. Garrison, *Thoughts on the African Colonization . . .* (Washington, 1835); William Jay, *An Inquiry into the Character and Tendency of the American Colonization and Anti-Slavery Societies* (New York, 1835); Edmund Ruffin, *The African Colonization Unveiled* (n.d); G. B. Stebbins, *Facts and Opinions Touching the Real Origin, Character, and Influence of the American Colonization Society . . .* (Boston, 1853); Charles Stuart, *A Memoir of Granville Sharpe* (New York, 1836).

[4]Tom W. Shick, *Behold the Promised Land: A History of Afro-American Settler Society in Nineteenth Century Liberia* (Baltimore, 1980), pp. 44-49, 73, 74, and 143.

[5]The main source relied upon is Walter Rodney, *A History of the Upper Guinea Coast, 1545-1800* (London, 1971), pp. 39-70. Several other works treat the subject of the ethnic character of pre-Liberia. Among the must useful are: Christopher Fyfe, *Sierra Leone Inheritance* (London, 1964), p. 43; Christopher Fyfe, "Peoples of the Windward Coast A.D. 100-1800," in J. F. Ade Ajayi and Ian Espie, eds., *A Thousand Years of West African History* (Ibadan, 1965), pp. 149-164; Svend Holsoe, "Slavery and Economic Response Among the Vai (Liberia and Sierra Leone)," in Suzanne Miers and Igor Kopytoff, eds., *Slavery in Africa: Historical and Anthropological Perspectives* (Madison, 1977), pp. 287-333; and N. W. Thomas, "Who Were the Manes?" *Journal of the African Society*, XIX (1919), pp. 176-188.

[6]Although it has been variously defined, the term under-development is considered in this work as an "inability of a social formation to make rational use of its natural and human resources." For the details of this definition see James H. Mittelman, *Underdevelopment and the Transition to Socialism: Mozambique and Tanzania* (New York, 1981), pp. 13-19.

CHAPTER I

THE AMERICAN COLONIZATION SOCIETY:

THE DETERMINANTS IN THE UNITED STATES

To understand the ACS and its effects on what became Liberia, it is essential to examine the origin of the organization and the social backgrounds of the individuals who played the leading roles in its formation and operations. The reason for this is simple: the backgrounds and the political, social, and religious beliefs of these men were to determine the overall activity of the ACS. Indeed, the legacy of the ACS which was passed on to Liberia was largely a synthesis of the social values, or norms, and beliefs of its founders.

The ACS was the product of a movement to promote the colonization of blacks outside the United States. This movement represented one alternative for coming to grips with what was, from at least the time of the Revolutionary War and the framing of the Republic, a basic American dilemma: the continuation of slavery in the very nation that had emphasized that "all men are created equal."[1]

Before America won its independence, many of its revolutionary leaders were quick to charge that the British crown was responsible for the continuation of slavery in America. Thomas Jefferson's early draft of the Declaration of Independence stipulated, for example, that George III:

> . . . has waged a cruel war against nature itself, violating its most sacred rights of life and liberty in the persons of a distant people who never offended him captivating and carrying them into slavery in another hemisphere or to incur miserable death on their transportation thither. This piratical

warfare, the opprobrium of infidel powers is the warfare of the Christian king of Great Britain. Determined to keep open a market where Men should be bought and sold, he has prostituted his negative for suppressing every legislative attempt to prohibit or to restrain this execrable commerce. . . .[2]

But the above sentences were later phased out of the Declaration. This was due to the pressure of those states which wanted the continuation of slavery in the United States.

It was partly against this background that the following compromises were made about the issue of slavery at the Constitutional Convention held in Philadelphia in 1787. It was agreed that slaves were to be considered property; a slave was to be counted as three fifths of a freeman. The slave trade was allowed to continue until 1808.[3] This constitutional arrangement was made to put to rest the political fight over slavery that existed between the slave and non-slaveholding states. But as a result of continued opposition to the arrangement from both sides and an unsuccessful slave revolt in Virginia in 1800,[4] it became evident that the compromises could not solve the issue of slavery. Accordingly, alternative solutions were increasingly suggested. One of these was the colonization of blacks in Africa.

By the end of the fourth decade of American independence, interest in the colonization movement had reached considerable proportions. Such influential figures as Jefferson, James Madison, and James Monroe supported the concept.[5] Strong interest and support led to the December 1816 founding, in Washington, D.C., of the ACS. Reorganized in January of 1817, the ACS became the most important instrument, though by no means the only one, for the realization of the colonization ideal.

Among the first prominent leaders of the ACS was Judge Bushrod Washington, a nephew of President George Washington. He served as first president of the ACS. Other leaders included William Crawford of Georgia, Henry Clay of Kentucky, John Howard, Samuel Smith, and John Smith all of Maryland, John Taylor of Virginia, John Mason of the District of Columbia, William Phillips of Massachusetts, Henry Rutgers of

New York, Robert Ralston of Pennsylvania and Samuel Bayard of New Jersey.[6] These served as the organization's first group of vice-presidents. An examination of membership lists in the annual reports of the ACS clearly indicates that most of the top positions in it were held by southerners.[7] This could particularly be said about the initial members of the Board of Managers whose main task was the formulation and implementation of the policies of the ACS. All but one of the first twelve members of the board were southerners.[8] It can therefore be maintained that the ACS was largely a southern initiative.[9]

To be precise, the ACS was principally an initiative of the uppermost economic and social group in the South. Briefly, southern society was stratified into several social groups. Those who owned plantations and large numbers of slaves composed the top layer of that social stratification. The members of this group were without a doubt the most influential men in the Old South. Their predominance was economically, socially, and politically manifested. Judge Washington, Clay, Crawford, Taylor, John C. Calhoun, and James Monroe, for example, were not only among the most wealthy men in the South, they were also among the political and social leaders of that region. They were also among the eminent leaders of the ACS.[10]

Indeed, their increasing interest and that of other southerners in the colonization initiative was heavily influenced by their deep involvement with the slave institution. Although they received their enormous social power and economic distinction through the owning of slaves and plantations, the members of the group were aware of the danger that was inherent in slavery and the potential for abolition. This feeling was reinforced as a result of an attempted slave revolt in 1800. As southerners, the founders and members of the ACS thus had a strong desire to protect the institution of slavery, and among the prominent reasons for that body's formation was, therefore, to mitigate the danger of further slave revolts and secure slavery.[11]

The colonization movement was, as a result, initially directed against the free blacks for it was generally held in the South that they were the main source of slave insurrections.[12] Free blacks were also characterized by many southern whites (as well as many in the North) as ignorant and criminal, a degraded people.[13] Free blacks, not slaves, were the group targeted for colonization.

While the desire to remove free blacks from the United States thus formed a powerful force behind the colonization movement, several contradictory motivations lay behind the promotion and defense of the movement. These may be seen in the arguments put forward by members and supporters of the ACS. Rev. John Randolph of Roanoke, Virginia, who saw the movement as a means of solving the slave issue and the promotion of missionary activities in Africa, was to argue that the ACS was not intended to undermine the slave institution but would help to safeguard the slaves of "every master in the United States."[14] Bishop William Meade of Virginia, who became a strong advocate of the ACS, put forward the position that while emancipated slaves would not be good Christians in America, they would be so in Africa. With this view, he recommended that colonization should be prerequisite for emancipation.[15] General Robert G. Harper, a large slaveholder, maintained that the ACS would bring benefit to America, since it was mainly designed to remove the "population for the most part that was idle and useless, and too often vicious and mischievous."[16] Bushrod Washington, the first president of the ACS, partly agreed with the foregoing proposition when he declared that the colonization initiative would "wipe from our political institutions the blot which stains them."[17]

In fact, nearly every early prominent member of the ACS emphasized that the movement was designed to secure slavery in America and promote Christianity and civilization in Africa.[18] It was held that free blacks were an undesirable element in America, but they would spread Christianity if sent to Africa. This was clearly spelled out by Clay at the first meeting of the ACS when he declared:

> Of all the classes of our population, the most vicious is that of the free colored. It is the inevitable result of their moral, political and evil degradation. Contaminated themselves, they extended their vices all around them, to the slaves, to the whites. Every emigrant to Africa is a missionary carrying the credentials in the holy cause of civilization, religion, and free institution.[19]

Obviously, these contradictory motives were influenced by the opposing forces over the issue of slavery. As most of the early colonizationists were southerners, they were heavily dependent on slavery as a mode of production. Just before the end of the American Civil War, for example, the total slave property was valued at about $300,000,000.[20] Besides, slavery was not only seen as an economic institution; it was also considered as a means of social control and a source of class respect.[21] With such vast interests at stake in the institution, southern colonizationists could not possibly afford to disassociate themselves easily from it.

But they were also fearful of the danger that was inherent in the institution. Indeed, the abolitionists' arguments that slavery was morally wrong and that the ACS was designed to perpetuate it, tended to affect the early colonizationists. They began, as a result, to associate the ACS with Christianity, civilization, and freedom. This was mainly emphasized to undermine the opposing forces and gain the support of every segment of American society. The African Repository, the main journal of the ACS, editorialized that:

> The object of the Colonization Society commends itself to every class of society. The landed proprieter may enhance the value of his property by assisting the enterprise. The patriot may contribute to the immortal honour of his country by generously relieving those whose degradation and misery in the midst of us, though a reproach, seems inevitable. . . . And what is more in character with the Christian profession than to enlighten the dark minds--to labour for the substantial and renown of one's country, and by deeds of noblest and most extensive charity to break the shackles of superstition and by conferring on civilized nations the freedom which is in Christ prepares them for an eternity. . . .[22]

This emphasis continued to characterize the ACS until after the Civil War. Following that conflict, only the organization's civilizing and missionary aspects were emphasized, since these were still appealing to most Americans.

Such divergent and contradictory opinions as those quoted above were indeed manifestations of the various social and religious views held by the eminent members of the ACS. Most of them were deeply religious, and in fact they were inclined to use religion to secure their social status and morally justify the social subordination of the dispossessed social groups.[23] This seems to partly explain why the ACS' scheme, which was initially directed against emancipated blacks, was labeled a divine undertaking that was to enlighten Africa, the place they were to colonize. No wonder the ACS' movement was seen as a positive aspect of slavery. This view corresponded with the "humanitarianism" the slaveholders associated with certain aspects of their paternalistic treatment of their slaves.[24]

One other inference can be gathered from these contradictory emphases: the ACS was not intended to be an imperial or economic venture. One searches the pages of the *African Repository* and the annual reports of the ACS in vain for references in support of colonization which make economic gain or national greatness for the United States their theme. These were obviously not substantial interests of the founders. Although these were not the main objectives of its leaders, the ACS' economic, political, social, and religious culture of paternalism which was inherited from the southern social environment, was to influence profoundly the political, economic, and religious formations of the Liberian colony the movement established.

As a synthesis of their institutional values, paternalism became the main ideology of the founders of the ACS. As has been argued by Professor David B. Davis, such an ideology as "an integrated system of beliefs, assumptions, and values not necessarily true or false," could be traced back to the Bible, the Greeks, the Romans, medieval and modern Europe, and colonial and early independent America.[25] The Bible sanctioned and "justified involuntary servitude and providence had assigned men to their proper social ranks."[26] This concept was advanced by Greek, Roman, and medieval scholars and promoted by later European theorists like John Locke, James Burgh, Thomas Hobbes, Samuel Pufendorf, and Francis Hutcheson.[27] Hobbes and Pufendorf agreed, for example, that most people "were governed by self-impulse, and that slavery was therefore a highly useful instrument of social discipline which might solve the problem of Europe's idlers, thieves, and vagabonds."

Locke recommended forced labor for the members of the underpriviledged class in British society. He reasoned that this would especially help to train the children of that society.[28] In Hutcheson's words:

> Nothing was so effectual as a perpetual bondage in prompting industry and restraining sloth, especially in the lower condition of society. . . . And that slavery should be the ordinary punishment of such idle vagrants. . . .[29]

The above ideology was borrowed, synthesized, and adapted to the Old South paternalistically.[30] Southern paternalism was heavily influenced by the foregoing concept; it preached that the slaveholding class could protect and be kind to the slaves and the poor whites in exchange for their social subordination and control. In fact, paternalism became the ideological core of the South because it met almost all the social requirements of its ruling class. With this concept, the members of the ruling class tended to view themselves as caretakers, the slaves as children, and the poor whites as lower class. But unlike the social subordination justified by the English theorists mentioned above, that of the South created a condition whereby nearly all the "fears and prejudices that had long been directed against the landless poor whites could not conveniently be confined" to the enslaved blacks.[31] It must be pointed out, however, that the idea of colonizing the free blacks in what became Liberia, because they were said to be dangerous in America, was similar to the English reason for deporting members of the poor class of England to the American colonies.[32]

As most of the early prominent members of the ACS were southern aristocrats, their social values were deeply influenced by paternalism. Doubtless, paternalism was a logical outcome of the class structure of the South. As suggested by Eugene D. Genovese, it was developed as a result of a need "to discipline and morally justify a system of exploitation and class subordination."[33] George Fitzhugh, one of the most influential theorists of the Old South, put it this way:

> It is the duty of society to protect the weak, but protection cannot be efficient without the power of control; therefore it is the duty of society to enslave the weak. And it is the duty which no organized and civilized society ever failed to

> perform. Parents, husbands, guardians, teachers, committees are masters under another name. . . .[34]

C. G. Memminger, another southern intellectual, maintained that "the slave institutions in the South increase the tendency to dignify the family. Each planter, in fact, is a patriarch of his household . . . . The fifth commandment becomes the foundation of society."[35]

Such an argument was not only held as an ideology in the Old South, but it was also put into practice in that region. Many slaveholders, especially those with large holdings, referred to their slaves as their "black families."[36] Some slaveholders went as far as recording the "births and deaths of their slaves in their family Bibles."[37] This practice as an aspect of paternalism was designed to ensure the submissiveness of the slaves and to secure and reinforce the patriarchal social domination of the masters. Those slaves who closely identified with the interests of their masters were rewarded with material things or appointed as leaders of their folks. They were the ones who usually became the "privileged slaves."[38]

Mulattoes could also be grouped in this social category, though for different reasons. Because they were offspring of the slave and master classes, the latter tended to be more receptive to them than the dark-skinned blacks. Of course this was part of the social legacy of the South which maintained that anything closer to the master class both in spirit and appearance would be more preferred to the one that was not.[39] This legacy was passed on through the ACS to the Liberian colony.

Despite this aspect of the tender heartedness of the "family government" of the Old South, it was quite harsh. Indeed, it had characteristics that were extremely oppressive and dehumanizing. The vast documentary evidence showing the severe beating of slaves, which in some cases left permanent scars on their bodies, attests to this.[41] The branding of slaves and the practice of "salt washing" of the wounds of slaves inflicted by the masters' lashes were among the most barbaric agonies imposed by the "family government." The most rebellious slave, when captured, was "ironed with shackles on each leg connected with a chain."[42] It has generally been held that the "whip was the most common instrument of punishment."[43] It also symbolized "the master's authority."[44] Like its humanitarian aspect, the oppressive nature of the "family government" was justified by Fitzhugh in this way:

> Two-thirds of mankind, the women and children are everywhere the subjects of family government. In all countries where slaves exist, the slaves also are the subjects of this kind of government. Now slaves, wives, and children have no other government; they do not directly come in contact with the institutions and rulers of the State. But the family government from its nature, has ever been despotic. The relations between the parent or master and his family subjects are too various, minute, and delicate to be arranged, defined, and enforced by law. God has in his mercy and wisdom provided a better check, to temper and direct the power of the family than any human government has devised.[45]

The charitable and tyrannical aspects of the "family government" which were indeed contradictory components of paternalism provided a convenient defense for the patriarchal, authoritative, aristocratic, and the exploitative social arrangements of the South, since it had Biblical sanction and certain "universal moral" attributes. These coupled with the fact that social oppression had been supported by some of the best world thinkers created a social concept whereby later generations accepted it as the natural order. Therefore, it is not surprising that the American slaveholding class, from which most of the early eminent members of the ACS emerged, viewed slavery, paternalism, and indeed the colonization scheme as God's designed plan.[46]

As already implied, paternalism was not only used as a social and religious means of control, it was also employed to facilitate the slave mode of production. Through paternalistic treatment, slaves were, for example, influenced to increase abundantly the wealth of their masters.[47] Of course when this aspect of paternalism failed, its oppressive aspect was quickly unleashed.[48] This feature of paternalism was influenced by the ACS and passed on to Liberia where it was modified by the representatives of the ACS in that colony.

The economic aspect of paternalism also supported certain social developments in the Old South. Its economic features shape an anti-egalitarian social organization.[49] Such features coincided with the patriarchal and aristocratic social arrangements of the South that were based on the slave mode of production. Had paternalism sustained equitable development in the South, the extreme monopolization of wealth and other social powers by the slaveholding class would have been inevitably undermined. Their enormous wealth, the main source of their social distinction, would have been apportioned among the masses of the South.[50]

This inequitable socio-economic development called into being certain attitudes or tendencies. As already noted, the members of the slaveholding class tended to treat their slaves paternalistically in return for their obedience and high labor output. Indeed, this pattern became an integral part of the slave mode of production. Although it tied the master and slave classes together, the slaveholders largely determined the relationship to ensure their domination. The slaves were coercively and persuasively influenced to depend on their masters for almost everything.[51] As will be examined, this dependent relationship that existed between the slaveholders and their slaves was inherited by the ACS and characterized its relationship with the black settlers it sent to Liberia.

But this dependent relationship not only prevailed between the slaveholders and slaves, it also existed between the former and the industrializing northern part of the United States. Unlike the relationship which existed between the slaves and their masters in the Old South, the one which existed between the Old South and the North took a more complex economic form. This complex economic link was largely determined by the North.

The reasons for the development of this unequal economic relationship between the South and North have been well treated in detail.[52] Most of the industrial and financial institutions in the United States during the period under consideration were based in the North. Just before the Civil War, seventy-five percent of the national wealth was held by the North. The North also controlled eighty-five percent of the nation's industries, and it owned about sixty-four percent of its total developed farm land. Indeed, most of America's national markets were in the North. This was due in considerable measure to the fact that the South had only about 9.1 million out of a total national population of 30.4 million, and 3.5 million of the South's figure constituted slaves.[53] With this in mind, it could be inferred that the net purchasing power of the South was smaller than that of the North. Even more was this the case since the patriarchal and aristocratic social arrangements together with the southern mode of production made it difficult for a relatively large middle class to emerge in that region. It has been maintained by Robert Starobin, for example, that:

> The slave development of southern industries stemmed partly from various restrictions on consumer demand. Slaveowners usually maintained their slaves at subsistence living standards . . . the poor whites lacked purchasing power because they did not produce for regional markets. . . . Southern transportation networks still primarily tied plantation districts to ports rather than providing a well knit system which might have increased internal consumption. Finally, the distribution propensities, was less even in the south than in the North.[54]

These socio-economic developments were no doubt largely the results of the economic system and social structures of the Old South. As already noted, the slaveholders could not afford to encourage the development of an egalitarian society or even a large middle class in their region. Inevitably, this would have undermined their social domination.

But they were not only concerned about their patriarchal or aristocratic social domination; they also were interested in outwardly expressing that domination and the social distinction that went with it. The slaveholders, especially those who owned large plantations, were inclined to build large houses with gothic designs. It has been maintained that "Southern planters" had an especial "taste for extravagant, wasteful display, causing [a] notorious lack of thrift and relative lack of economic development compared to that experienced in the North and West."[55] This assertion is sustained by Kenneth Stampp's observation that "during the early nineteenth century, thriftless Virginia planters still hired tutors for their children, surrounded themselves with an army of servants, and entertained on a grand scale." He went on to add that "it was not slavery itself but the Southern culture that required these extravagances."[56]

While southern mode of production, social manifestations, and consuming patterns helped to reinforce the social uniqueness of the slaveholders, they also ensured the dependent southern economic situation. This was all the more so since the South's slave mode of production and the social values called into being by it did not allow for the emergence of a self-sustaining economic initiative that would have accommodated a large number of the people in that region.[57]

But it would be mistaken to argue that southern social arrangements were the only contributing factors to the region's dependency. As already noted, the North largely determined the economic relationship that existed between it and the South. This was enhanced by the fact that the economic institutions and industries which regulated the relationship were mostly based in the North, and owned by the northerners. Thus they tended to determine the relationship on their behalf. Starobin maintains:

> Credit arrangements and unfavorable balances of trade drained plantation profits northward and permitted northern merchants increasingly to dominate the commerce in cotton, the leading export of both the South and of the nation. . . . The South would have to pay for loans and services obtained from the North in any event, but capital accumulated by northern merchants, bankers, and insurance brokers tended to be reinvested in northern industries, rather than in southern ones.[58]

Professors Alfred H. Conrad and John Meyer agree with the foregoing argument when they state that southern wealth might "have been drained . . . through the excessive use of credit. . . . The dependence upon advances was in fact a dependence upon the New York or London money market, and was an impediment to the accumulation of capital in the South."[59]

Although it rewarded the North more than the South, this economic relationship served the members of the slaveholding class in one crucial way: it continued to provide them with the necessary resources that helped to ensure their social supremacy and distinction up to the time of the Civil War. It could thus be accurately maintained that the slaveholders' economic dependence on the North was compensated for by their social, economic, and political domination of their slaves and the poor whites of the South. Although the process was not always harmonious up to the 1860s, it was no wonder they tended to accommodate the economic domination of the northern industrialists and bankers.[60]

The discussion so far clearly shows that southern society from which most of the prominent members of the ACS emerged was not a simple one. The economic dependent relationship that subordinately tied the South to the North and the one that existed between the slaveholding and dispossessed classes of the South together with the patriarchal or aristocratic social arrangements, the ideological and religious justifications called into being by these social formations were indeed part of the complex society of the South. As noted, the impact of these institutional developments on the South and ACS cannot be underestimated. In fact, it is only against these social backgrounds that the ACS and the Liberian colony that movement established can be thoroughly understood.

One aspect of the foregoing discussion was quickly manifested after the ACS was reorganized in 1817. Like most prestigious positions in the South, all the key positions of the newly formed organization were held by people with large slaveholdings. Judge Bushrod Washington, the first president, and most of the first group of vice-presidents were not only large slaveholders, but they were also prominent politicians or significant social leaders in the South. This statement could well be applied to most of the early eminent supporters of the ACS.[61] Lesser positions in the organization were usually occupied by smaller slaveholders.[62]

In addition, the top office holders called paternalistically and repeatedly upon the white masses to support the ACS' initiative.[63] Increasingly, the ACS became dependent on this group for both material and spiritual support. A person of this group who demonstrated devotion to the cause of the ACS was allowed to play a leadership role in the movement. Indeed, most of the leaders of the local divisions of the ACS were from this group.[64]

This opportunity was not, however, extended to the blacks who were the most oppressed social group in the South. In contrast to the abundant documentary evidence that whites from the lesser property holding class held positions lower down in the ACS' hierarchy, there is no single record of any blacks in similar positions.[65] What was required of them was not leadership or membership in the ACS but a willingness to go to West Africa where they would promote the ACS' concept of civilization. This concept, of course, meant the promotion of southern political, economic, religious and other institutional values in Africa. This was the southern legacy of the ACS. In addition, the blacks were told that only in West Africa could they enjoy full freedom.[66]

Nevertheless, it required more than the existence of the ACS and its appeal to blacks to make the colonization initiative a reality; support of the United States government was an obvious necessity. The leaders of the ACS recognized this from the first, and in March 1819 their lobbying efforts bore fruit in congressional action which would have a positive impact on colonization efforts.[67] Congress passed legislation which empowered President Monroe:

> To provide for the safekeeping and removal from the United States of all Negroes captured from foreign slave traders, and to appoint agents to receive them on the coast of West Africa.[68]

A sum not to exceed $100,000 was set aside to carry out this task.[69]

With this action and his increasing personal interest in the colonization movement, President Monroe promptly decided to appoint an agent from among the officials of the ACS to represent the federal government's interests. The agent was authorized to use the funds provided by the United States government to send the recaptives, or slaves who had been smuggled into the United States but had not yet experienced plantation slavery, back to West Africa. A similar agent was appointed to receive the recaptives in what became the Liberian colony in 1822.[70]

Given this boost, the ACS' colonization initiative went forward rapidly. It took an initial step towards the formation of a West African colony in January 1820 when a group of black settlers and their white ACS' representatives started to sail from New York City for the West African coast. This began the conveying process by which the ACS' institutional values were carried to Liberia. The effects of those values on what became Liberia as a result of this process were to be immense.

As Liberia took shape in the nineteenth century, it would come to reflect the values of the founders and leading supporters of the ACS. These were very much the political, social, economic, and religious beliefs and norms of the slaveholding class of the Old South. To better understand the the impact of these on that portion of the West African coast that became Liberia, it is necessary to examine first the African society of that region.

NOTES

Chapter I

[1]Matthew T. Mellon, *Early American Views on Negro Slavery* (New York, 1969), p. v.

[2]*Ibid.*, pp. 97-98.

[3]*Ibid.*, pp. 68-69.

[4]Henry N. Sherwood, "Early Negro Deportation Projects," *Mississippi Valley Historical Review, II* (1916), pp. 484-495.

[5]Mellon, *Early American Views*, 153-159. George Livermore, *An Historical Research Respecting the Opinions of the Founding Fathers of the Republic on Negroes as Slaves, as Citizens, and as Soldiers,* (Boston, 1863, p. 93; see also the following works: H. A. Washington, ed., *The Writings of Thomas Jefferson*, Vol. III (New York, 1904); and Gaillard Hunt, ed., *The Writings of James Madison*, Vol. III (New York, 1910), pp. 135-136.

[6]*First Annual Report of the ACS* (1818), p. 11.

[7]*Fifth Annual Report of the ACS* (1822), p. 5.

[8]Jay, *An Inquiry into the Character and Tendency*, p. 11.

[9]Bancroft goes so far as to say that the men representing northern states "were only figureheads." Bancroft, "The Colonization of American Negroes, 1816-1865," p. 157.

[10]The social backgroundsof the prominent founders of the ACS have been treated in detail in the following works: *Ibid.*; Fox, *The American Colonization Society*; Staudenraus, *The African Colonization Movement*; Opper, "The Minds of the White Participants; "Eli Seifman, "A History of;" Sherwood, "The Formation of the American Colonization Society;" Foster, "The Colonization of Free Negroes in Liberia;" and Wickstron, "The American Colonization and Liberia."

[11]Bancroft, "The Colonization of American Negroes, 1816-1865," pp. 155-156.

[12]*Ibid.*, and Alexander, *A History of Colonization*, p. 87.

[13]This was supported, for example, by data which purported to show that blacks constituted a large proportion of the prison inmates in the United States. *African Repository and Colonial Journal* (hereafter *African Repository*), II (1826), pp. 152-154; *African Repository*, V (1829), p. 276.

[14]*A View of Exertions Lately Made for the Purpose of Colonizing the Free People of Color in Africa or Elsewhere* (Washington, 1817), p. 30.

[15]John John, *A Memoir of the Life of the Right Reverend William Meade*, pp. 476-477.

[16]*First Annual Report of the ACS* (1818), p. 30.

[17]*Ibid.*

[18]Jay, *An Inquiry into the Character and Tendency*, pp. 95-111.

[19]*Tenth Annual Report of the ACS* (1826), pp. 21-22.

[20]Kenneth Stampp, *The Era of Reconstruction* (New York, 1965), p. 57.

[21]Ulrich B. Phillips, *American Negro Slavery* (Baton Rouge, 1918), pp. 291-308, 489-490.

[22]*African Repository*, I (1825), p. 67.

[23]The ways in which this was done with black slaves have been well treated in Kenneth M. Stampp, *The Peculiar Institution: Slavery in the Ante-Bellum South* (New York, 1956), pp. 156-162.

[24]*Ibid.*, pp. 322-330; Eugene D. Genovese, *The World the Slaveholders Made* (new York, 1969), pp. 97,99-100.

[25]David B. Davis, *The Problem of Slavery in the Age of Revolution, 1770-1823* (Ithaca, 1975), p. 14.

[26]Robert R. Palmer, *The Age of the Democratic Revolution: A Political History of Europe and America, 1760-1800* (Princeton, 1959), pp. 387-396.

[27]Davis, *The Problem of Slavery*, pp. 261, 263. See also the following works about this argument: _______, *The Problem of Slavery in Western Culture* (Ithaca, 1969); Marcus W. Jernegan, "Slavery and Conversion in the American Colonies," *American Historical Review*, XXI (1916); Abdel-Mohsen Bakir, *Slavery in Pharaonic Egypt* (Cairo, 1952); Glenn R. Morrow, *Plato Law of Slavery in Relation to Greek Law* (Urbana, 1939); and Robert Schlaifer, "Greek Theories of Slavery from Homer to Aristotle," *Harvard Studies in Classical Philology*, XLVII (1936).

[28]Davis, *The Problem of Slavery in the Age*, p. 263.

[29]Quoted in *Ibid.*, pp. 263-264.

[30]Eugene D. Genovese, *Roll Jordan Roll: The World the Slaves Made* (New York, 1976), pp. 5-7.

[31]Davis, *The Problem of Slavery in the Age*, p. 261.

[32]Edmund S. Morgan, "Slavery and Freedom: The American Paradox," *The Journal of American History*, LIX (1972), pp. 6,25,29.

[33]Genovese, *Roll Jordan Roll*, p. 4.

[34]Quoted in C. Vann Woodward, ed., George Fitzhugh, *Cannibals All or Slaves Without Masters* (Cambridge, 1973), p. 187.

[35]William Jenkins, *Pro-Slavery Thought in the Old South* (Chapel Hill, 1935), p. 210.

[36]Genovese, *The World the Slaveholders Made*, p. 196.

[37]Caryle Sitterman, *Sugar Country: The Sugar Industry in the South, 1753-1950* (Lexington, 1955), p. 96. See these works also: Winthrop Jordan, *White Over Black: American Attitudes Toward the Negroe, 1550-1812* (Baltimore, 1968); Stampp, *The Peculiar Institution*; Ira Berlin, *Slaves without Masters: The Free Negro in the Antebellum South*(New York, 1974).

[38]For detailed treatment of this argument see these works: Berlin, *Slaves Without Masters*; Stampp, *The Peculiar Institution*; Jordan, *White Over Black*; James Oakes, *The Ruling Race: History of American Slaveholders* (New York, 1983); Genovese, *The World the Slaveholders Made*; and Michael Johnson and James L. Roark, *Black Masters: A Free Family of Color in the Old South* (New York, 1984).

[39]Johnson and Roark, *Black Masters*, p. 97; Oakes, *The Ruling Race*, pp. 48-49; Jordan, *White Over Black*, pp. 167-69; and Stampp, *The Peculiar Institution*, pp. 339-340.

[40]Most large slaveholders felt that the authority they had over their slaves was a kind of family government and was not therefore as oppressive as the abolitionists tended to picture. For this emphasis see, Woodward, ed., *George Fitzhugh, Cannibals All* and Phillips, *American Negro Slavery*.

[41]Stampp, *The Peculiar Institution*, p. 174.

[42]James Coleman, *Slavery Times in Kentucky* (Chapel Hill, 1940), pp. 248-49.

[43]Stampp, *The Peculiar Institution*, p. 174.

[44] *Ibid.*

[45] George Fitzhugh, *Sociology for the Old South or the Failure of Free Society* (Richmond, 1854), p. 105.

[46] Genovese, *The World the Slaveholders Made*, pp. 151-164; ______, *Roll Jordan Roll*, pp. 3-7; Oakes, *The Ruling Race*. pp. 97-122; for the colonization aspect, see Bancroft, "Colonization of the American Negroes, 1816-1865,".

[47] Stammp, *The Peculiar Institution*, pp. 163-170.

[48] *Ibid.*, pp. 171-177.

[49] For detailed treatments of this explanation see the following works: Genovese, *The World the Slaveholders Made*; Oakes, *The Ruling Race*; and Phillips, *American Negro Slavery*.

[50] It appears that this was what happened during the Civil War. The war weakened the social supremacy of the slaveholding class. The conflict destroyed the main source of power of that class, which was slavery. But the former slaveholders did, however, manage to reestablish their social hegemony in the South after 1877. For detailed treatment of this argument see these works: Stampp, *The Era of Reconstruction* and Berlin, *Slaves Without Masters*.

[51] Stampp, *The Peculiar Institution*, pp. 147-148, 162-170,171-177.

[52] See particularly these works: Alfred H. Conrad and John R. Meyer, "The Economics of Slavery in the Ante-Bellum South," in Gerald D. Nash, ed., *Issues in American Economic History* (Boston, 1966), pp. 274-280; Robert S. Starobin, *Industrial Slavery in the Old South* (New York, 1971), pp. 187-189; Eugene D. Genovese, *The Political Economy of Slavery* (New York, 1961).

[53] John O'Sullivan and Edward Keuchel, *American Economic History: From Abundance to Constraint* (New York, 1981), pp. 87-89.

[54]Starobin, *Industrial Slavery*, pp. 186-187.

[55]Conrad and Meyer, "The Economics of Slavery," p. 270.

[56]Stampp, *The Peculiar Institution*, p. 391.

[57]Conrad and Meyer, "The Economics of Slavery," p. 270.

[58]Starobin, *Industrial Slavery*, p. 187.

[59]Conrad and Meyer, "The Economics of Slavery," p. 270.

[60]For the various occasional oppositions to northern economic domination of the South before the Civil War, see the following works: Charles and Mary Beard, "The Tariff as a Cause of Sectional Strife and the Civil War," in Nash, ed., *Issues in American Economic History*, pp. 274-280; and Richard Hofstadter, "The Tariff Issue on the Eve of the Civil War," in *Ibid.*, pp. 280-285.

[61]Bancroft, "The Colonization of American Negroes, 1816-1865," pp. 155-156.

[62]Fox, *The American Colonization*, p. 51; and Jay, *An Inquiry into the Character and Tendency*, p. 11.

[63]*African Repository*, V (1830), p. 383; and Bancroft, "The Colonization of American Negroes, 1816-1865," p. 171.

[64]This aspect of the ACS is detailed in Fox's, *The American Colonization*. See also *Second Annual Report of the ACS* (1818), pp. 132-142; and the *African Repository*, I (1825), pp. 222-224.

[65]See these works for this explanation: Bancroft, "The Colonization of American Negroes, 1816-1865,"; Sherwood, "The Formation of the American Colonization Society,"; and Philip Slaughter, *The Virginia History of African Colonization* (Richmond, 1855).

[66]*Ibid.*

[67] *Third Annual Report of the ACS* (1819), pp. 43-45.

[68] Bancroft, "The Colonization of American Negroes, 1816-1865," p. 164.

[69] *Third Annual Report of the ACS*, p. 46.

[70] Bancroft, "The Colonization of American Negroes, 1816-1865," p. 164.

CHAPTER II

PRE-COASTAL LIBERIA: THE PEOPLES AND THEIR ENVIRONMENT BEFORE 1822[1]

Just as it is essential to understand the social background of the ACS, so it is crucial to examine the social organization of coastal pre-Liberian society. This is needed to provide a comparative understanding of the former and the latter before examining their effects on the Liberian colony in greater detail.

Before Liberia was established in 1822, that area had already been affected by both internal and external forces. The Manes' invasions came from the interior of what became the Ivory Coast and Ghana. The invasions began in 1545, and by 1560 their effects had been felt by nearly all the major ethnic groups of coastal pre-Liberia and those of coastal pre-Sierra Leone. As these invasions involved successful military actions, the Manes were able to impose their values on those they had defeated. By 1567, the leaders of the invaders had partitioned the coastal area of pre-Sierra Leone among themselves, forming several kingdoms.[2] At a subsequent level, petty rulers were appointed. In a way, the Manes succeeded in introducing on the West African coast a political culture that reflected a "pyramidical structure of government. . . ."[3]

The overlord of the foregoing political arrangement resided at Cape Mount. He was able to control his subjects not only by military force but also by setting one ethnic group against another. Hence, by the seventeenth century, his presence had been deeply felt on the coast of what became Liberia. During this period, for example, he forced the defeated people to pay tributes to him.[4]

Almost concurrent with the invasions of the Manes was the arrival of the Vai ethnic group in the Cape Mount region. The Vais were among the Africans who made up the nucleus of the Malian Empire.[5] But as the Malian Empire collapsed in the fourteenth century, they were forced to migrate to the coast of pre-Liberia.[6] The disruption of the northern salt trade seems to have influenced their exodus to the south. Another force that might have led to their migration was their taste for kola nuts; kola producing trees grew in the forests around the Cape Mount region.[7]

By 1600, the Vais had reached the Cape Mount area. But this development precipitated a reaction from other Africans such as the Kru and other ethnic groups of the region. They formed an alliance to arrest the advance of the Vais. The Manes exploited this conflict by joining the alliance. Because of this united front, the Vais were finally defeated, though they were allowed to remain in the Cape Mount region.[8]

The settlement of the Vais along the Mano River provided them with a trading opportunity, and they were quick to take advantage of this. They began immediately, for example, to serve as middlemen between the Dutch traders stationed on the Cape Mount coast, and the interior Africans. Initially, they exchanged "legitimate" African products for European guns, gun powder, rum, etc. But the trade in "legitimate" goods was modified as the European traders began increasingly to demand slaves in exchange for their goods. Indeed, by the beginning of the nineteenth century, the Vais were among the leading African slavers in the Gallinas and Cape Mount regions.[9]

The above activity was not only confined to the Vais; it was also practiced by other coastal pre-Liberian Africans such as the Kru and the Glebo. The Kru, like the Vais, have been considered as a subgroup of the Mane-speaking peoples. If one agrees with this argument, then the Kru might have arrived at their present location by the middle of the sixteenth century.[10] Their basic political formation was patrimonial; power usually was derived from one's father or male ancestor. With this, the Kru political formation seems to have been centralized. But because of "political or demographic" pressure, the Kru centralized and relatively large political unit broke up into smaller ones.[11] Although there was a sentiment of one cultural nation, the various Kru political units seem to have been in competition with each other.[12] As some of the political units became increasingly independent, they tended to develop as different cultural units as well.[13] This seems to explain why scholars continue to be confused about whether the Carou were a subgroup of the Kru.[14] This confusion could also be applied to other African groups who were affected by the Manes' invasions.[15]

As noted, the Kru were also involved with the Atlantic trade. Their involvement probably began in the seventeenth century. It started as follows:

> At first . . .[Kru] traders became agents at particular places along the coast by using recommendations provided by previous European employers. Slowly this practice evolved into a system whereby such individuals, with a couple of friends and their canoes, would be taken on board a European ship and used as trading intermediaries along a longer stretch of the coast. Later these individuals were either returned to their places of origin, or were put off on the coast with their canoes to paddle their own way home.[16]

The employment of Kru on European ships has been well documented.[17] Early Kru labor recruits came mainly from the Settra coastal area of pre-Liberia. Kru laborers worked at Freetown, Sierra Leone, and nearly all other major European trading outposts on the coast of what became Liberia. Their main tasks were not only the loading and unloading of European ships; they also served as laborers on European plantations in Sierra Leone and later on in the construction of the Suez and Panama Canals.[18] In fact, during the nineteenth century, Kru laborers could be found on nearly every major plantation in West Africa. Later in the twentieth century, about 800 Kru laborers were employed on Spanish plantations on Fernando Po Island.[19]

Besides their involvement with these activities, the Kru were also involved with the "legitimate" trade and later the slave trade. The first information on the purchasing of ivory a Kru coastal trading bought fish from the region. It is not known, however, whether these items were bought from the Kru Africans, since accounts of the transaction only described the Africans as fishermen. Nevertheless, a later description clearly spelled out the Africans who were involved in the transaction and the goods in which they traded.

> The commerce of the Kroomen is carried on entirely by barter, as they have no fixed medium of exchange. Articles which are in greatest demand among them are tobacco, cotton cloth, East India fabric, a few English shawls and hats, leather trunks, firearms, bar-iron which they manufactured themselves into implements of husbandry, knives, cowries, which are used in making fetishes or amulets. In return for these articles they sold a little ivory, palm oil, Malaguetta pepper, and rice, and occasionally supplied ships with firewood, plantains, cassava and even bullocks.[20]

By the 1820s, the Kru exchanged their items for the following European goods: "kettles and pans, pewter basins, looking glasses, beads, mugs, gun flints, rum, trade checks, blankets, spoons, and drums."[21] As will be noted, Kru involvement with the Atlantic trade was to have a profound effect on their social formations.

Most of the descriptions put forward so far could be applied to the Glebo ethnic group who inhabited the southeastern tip of pre-Liberia. Like the Vais and Kru, the Glebo are said to have been affected by the Manes' invasions.[22] The invasions seem to have forced the Glebo to migrate to the coast of what became Liberia. During their migration, the Glebo came into contact with other ethnic groups such as the Tuobo, Nyinebo, Webo, Gweabo, Bakwe, and Palibo who still dwell in the western part of the Ivory Coast. This explains why it has been argued that the cultural values of these groups are nothing but a synthesis of the previous cultural values of the groups. In fact, these peoples have been categorized as a Kru-speaking group.[23]

The effect of these interactions did not only lead to a similarity of the languages spoken by the groups, it also affected their religions. It has been maintained, for example, that these ethnic groups all considered Mount Tyeyle, located in eastern Liberia, as a home for their dead.[24] Indeed, some of the groups who lived as far away as what became Ghana made "sacrifices" to a god that was resident on the southeastern coast of Liberia.[25] No wonder the Sapa and Tie ethnic groups of the Ivory coast continue to accept the Glebo god, Kuu, as their god.[26]

The brief descriptions of the Vais, Kru, and the Glebo suggest one important thing: that the three ethnic groups were being acted upon by forces as they came into contact with the Europeans and later the ACS. These forces were, of course, the various ethnic groups involved, and the physical environs of the wide area they inhabited. Their interactions with each other and with their environments set into motion transitional processes that continued to influence or characterize their various social formations. These ongoing social changes were reinforced by the activities of the European traders and the ACS on the coastal area of what became Liberia. To understand this, it is necessary first to examine in detail the activities of the European traders and their effects on the social formations of the region under study.

As is well known, the overseas expansion that brought the Europeans into direct contact with the coast of West Africa began in 1415 when the Portuguese captured Ceuta in what became part of modern Morocco.[27] Following this, they started to sail south along the coast of West Africa. Hence, Cape Blanco was reached in 1441, and a few years later, the coast of pre-Sierra Leone was surveyed by a Portuguese named Pedro da Sintra. In fact, the Portuguese were acquainted with the coastal area between Ceuta and Sierra Leone by 1462.[28]

The Portuguese and other European involvement with the Grain Coast[29] (see map p. 78) began after they had established the Elmina trading post on the Gold Coast. Although they started trading with the Africans who inhabited the Grain Coast in 1515,[30] the Europeans did not establish themselves on the mainland at this time. This was due to the following factors: the fear that they might be kidnapped or enslaved by the Africans and the fact that there were no good natural sea ports on the Grain Coast. Because of these obstacles, the European traders were forced to remain at sea and conducted their trading transactions with the mainland through African intermediaries.[31]

But by the end of the 1500s, nevertheless, the Europeans were increasingly involving themselves with the Grain Coast products as the Malaguetta pepper, ivory, camwood, wax, gold, and later slaves. Indeed, by 1602 the Dutch had established a trading outpost at Cape Mount, on the southwestern part of the Grain Coast, to protect what they imagined as an important "gold trade" route to the interior.[32] Later, the Dutch

Malaguetta pepper, ivory, camwood, wax, gold, and later slaves. Indeed, by 1602 the Dutch had established a trading outpost at Cape Mount, on the southwestern part of the Grain Coast, to protect what they imagined as an important "gold trade" route to the interior.[32] Later, the Dutch developed a sugar cane plantation in the area. The plantation was, however, destroyed by an African chief who was inspired by his Afro-Portuguese brother. The latter feared that the presence of the Dutch increasingly threatened his trading interest. This did not, however, force the Dutch to abandon the area. Still, by 1616 their presence was well evident; they continued to trade at other places along the West African coast.[33]

Like the Portuguese and Dutch, the English began to interest themselves increasingly in the Grain Coast trade. By the beginning of the seventeenth century, they had established two trading outposts along the coast not too far from Cape Mount. The two outposts were, however, controlled by African rulers to whom the English paid rents.[34] By this means, an English firm, Wood and Company, traded at the Sherbro and Cape Mount areas for about twenty-five years. The trade mainly involved camwood which was in great demand in Europe and at European trading out-posts in West Africa.[35] In fact, Sherbro Island (see map p. 104) became the main English West African trading base; from there they expanded their trading initiatives to other coastal regions.[36]

Having established trading stations on the coast of West Africa, the Europeans increasingly intensified their trading activities in that region. The European trade started with non-human cargo. These goods included "gold, ivory, beeswax, camwood, pepper, hides, resin, pelts, civet, ambergis, cotton, soap, raffia mats, palm oil, rice, millet, and citrus fruit."[37] These items were usually bartered for such European goods as cloth, hats, rum, and copper bracelets. During the early 1500s, the Portuguese accumulated about "5000 doubloons of good gold" from West Africa. The amount mainly came from the area around what became known as the Gambia. This achievement, and the exaggeration that characterized it, impelled the British and later the French to intensify their interests in the West African trade.[38] It must be pointed out, however, that the exaggeration that gold was abundant in West Africa played a more influential role in the European expansion in the area than the gold that was really available there.[39] The recognition of this forced the Europeans, especially the Portuguese, to develop an interest in other West African produce.

The most important West African products which began to capture the attention of the Portuguese, English, and Dutch traders were ivory, beeswax, camwood, and slaves. In 1551, the Portuguese gathered a large amount of ivory from the mainland and sent it to Cape Verde for shipment to Europe. By 1582, the English and the Dutch were deeply involved in the ivory trade. Andre de Faro, a Portuguese missionary, described the English and Dutch involvement in the ivory trade in 1664:

> Before my eyes, they loaded 28,000 teeth, many of which weighed four *arrobas*, some weighed six *arrobas*, and there were numerous smaller ones. Every year a ship comes to take a smaller cargo. Judge from this how many elephants were killed here every year, because each one has only two teeth, thus 14,000 elephants must be slain annually. This does not take account of the ivory that is purchased in the other rivers of Guinea, where there are similar factories which dispatch other ships; and the Dutch are also buyers in the ports of these rivers. There are therefore more elephants in Guinea than there are cattle in the whole of Europe.[40]

This increasing demand for ivory was to lead to reduction of the number of elephants in the area under study. In fact, this was what happened to the Cape Mount region where elephants were once plentiful.[41]

Beeswax was also exported from West Africa, but in small quantity. Most of the beeswax was taken from the coast of Gambia. A relatively large amount was taken from that region in the sixteenth century. The three registered European ships that were mainly involved with the trade of the area each carried 400 "quintals of wax annually."[42]

As mentioned, camwood was another item which reinforced Europeans' involvement with the coast of West Africa. During 1678,

Wood and Company employed local Africans to establish a camwood "factory" near Cape Mount. Most of the wood used in the "factory" came from the interior where forest trees were abundant. In 1682, it was reported that "seventeen tons of camwood" from the vicinities of Sherbro and Cape Mount were exported to London. In December of the same year, about 197 tons of camwood were prepared for possible shipment overseas.[43]

Although Europeans' interest in these goods did not immediately diminish when the transatlantic slave trade was introduced, that trade finally succeeded in subordinating the significance of the trade in the former goods. This process accelerated when the New World began to make increasing demands for African labor to serve its tobacco, indigo, rice, and cotton plantations and silver and gold mines.[44] Hence, this labor demand was to have a lasting impact on the social evolution of coastal West Africa. To understand this, it is necessary to reassert the introduction and the effects of the trade on the coast of West Africa.

Like the "legitimate" trade, the transatlantic slave trade was started by the Portuguese and then taken up by other Europeans such as Spaniards, Dutch, French, Danes, and English.[45] By 1494, the Portuguese were given papal sanction for their claim of the entire African continent.[46] Before this, they had already established trading outposts at Ceuta and Elmina. Indeed, slaves from the coast of Guinea were sent to Lisbon in 1518. But the need for African labor in Portugal, or in other European countries, was not so great as to require the enslavement of a large number of Africans.[47] It was the New World, however, that offered a demanding alternative for Africans.

By 1518, King Charles V of Spain and Portugal had given a special license to shippers to carry four thousand Africans to the Spanish colonies in the West Indies.[48] This prompted other European merchants to appeal to their leaders to offer them a similar opportunity. It could, therefore, be maintained that the trade which was started by the Portuguese and inherited by the Spaniards had become significant by the end of the 1500s.

Between 1562 and 1640, Portugal and Spain jointly issued licenses that authorized shippers to transport from one hundred to six hundred slaves at a time to the West Indies. As the regulation of ships for tax collecting purposes became more efficient, a ship could transport from four to five hundred slaves to the New World. By 1590, about three thousand slaves had been exported from one area in the Upper Guinea.[49]

The Manes' invasions that affected the coast of pre-Liberia corresponded with the advance of the Atlantic slave trade to the coast of West Africa. The Portuguese were to take advantage of the social disruptions brought to the coastal societies by the invasions. When in 1545 some Portuguese "ocean-going slavers" learned of the war that was being fought between the Manes and Sapes, they decided, for example, to exploit the situation by sending a number of boats to the main area of the conflict. The objective of this pursuit was to enslave those who were defeated. Fortunately for the Portuguese, there were many such victims to load their ships to capacity.[50]

Obviously, the Manes' invasions coincided with the needs of the Atlantic slave trade. It has been argued that the Manes, in effect, began to view the supply of slaves to "the Europeans as an end in itself." During the 1580s, for example, the Manes' leader, King Farma, could provide, if asked, three to four hundred slaves to European slavers by going to war.[51] Indeed, human stealing became common on the pre-Liberian coast, especially by the late 1600s. Of the 5.6 million slaves taken by the British from the Windward Coast[52] between 1690 and 1807, about 300,000 came directly from the area of what became Liberia.[53] As will be illustrated, this involuntary migration was to affect the societies of the region.

Thus, it should be emphasized in describing these developing commercial relationships that when the Europeans first met the people of the West African coast, the former's main objective was trade, not territorial conquest or domination. Although the British occupied two trading outposts on the Grain coast, these outposts were not owned by them. They were rented from African rulers. Indeed, up to the eighteenth century, the Africans continued to have complete sovereignty over the region.[54]

This contact, however, was, to set into motion an historical process that was not traditional to coastal West Africa. The payment of rents to African leaders by European traders attests to this. In fact, it could be argued that this was the origin of the "making" of illegitimate chiefs; illegitimate in the sense that these chiefs, especially the coastal ones, unlike the earlier leaders, were beginning to rely increasingly on European goods and trading privileges as the main sources of political power. In the process, they were conditioned to accept new values and norms. The values in question included the use or consumption of European goods such as European chairs, tables, cloths, hats, knives, guns and gunpowder, rum, and tobacco. Besides, coastal chiefs were forced to learn *Krio*, a combination of English, French, Portuguese, Spanish, and coastal West African languages. Those who succeeded in doing this were not only easily accommodated by the transatlantic trade, they were also viewed by the Europeans as the legitimate leaders of their people.[55]

But as already implied, the means of acquiring these values were to have poignant rather than superficial effects on the coastal societies of West Africa. The effects of the transatlantic slave trade on the coast of West Africa bears testimony to this proposition. It has been generally accepted, for instance, that about fifteen million Africans were taken from Africa to the New World by the trade. As noted, some 300,000 slaves from this number came directly from the area of pre-Liberia.[56]

Like other West African coastal regions, that of Liberia was thus affected by the foregoing labor demand. Coastal ethnic groups like the Vais would, for example, invade the interior mainly to capture slaves for European slavers who waited on the coast. Moreover, the practice of domestic slavery that was part of the social formation of the Vais was modified to meet the labor demand of the New World. Like their European counterparts, the Vai slavers began to view their slaves as marketable objects. In fact, this became pronounced when they became the major suppliers of slaves from the Cape Mount region.[57]

As with the social formation of the Vais, that of the Kru was affected by the Atlantic trade. The inception of Kru coastal trading outposts or towns coincided, for instance, with their increasing involvement with the Atlantic trade. Indeed, these coastal outposts or towns became the first recruitment centers of Kru laborers. From the beginning of the 1500s up to the middle of the 1800s, the Kru were said to be the major suppliers of slaves on the coastal area of pre-Liberia. They assisted the notorious Spanish slaver, Don Pedro Blanco, who had slave stations on the pre-Liberian coast.[58] It was rumored that the Kru continued to trade in human beings even after Liberia was established. A European reported in 1840 that the Kru had about 1500 slaves in their baracoon ready for overseas shipment.[59] The Kru were also busy buying slaves at Cape Mount for their European counter-parts in 1848.[60]

Although their active involvement with the trade provided them with material rewards, it also affected their institutional developments. This was clearly illustrated by a nineteenth century account of the ways in which the newly acquired wealth was appropriated:

> A certain portion is given to the headman of the town; all of his relatives and friends partake of his bounty, if there be but a leaf of tobacco for each; his mother, if living, has a handsome present. All of this is done to get him a good name: what remains is delivered to his father to buy him a wife. One so liberal does not long want a partner: the father obtains a wife for him; and after a few months of ease and indulgence he sets off afresh for Sierra Leone or some of the factories on the coast to get more money. By this he is proud of being acquainted with white man's fashion; he takes with him some raw inexperienced youngster whom he initiated into his own profession. . . . In this way he proceeds perhaps for ten or twelve years or more, increasing the number of wives, and establishing a great character among his countrymen.[61]

Evidently, this new social formation was called into being largely by the Atlantic trade. The official function of the Kru *gbaubi* or "father of the army," which was traditionally "military in nature," was modified to meet the needs of the Atlantic trade. The new role of *gbaubi* became a kind of supervisory task of the new Kru labor force required by the trade. Hence, the Kru labor force, which was initially nothing but "an amorphous band of laborers" was later reorganized into an efficient work force to load and unload European ships. By the early 1800s, another new administrative position was created among the Kru. A Kru headman was appointed to "keep order" and to negotiate with the Europeans on behalf of his people. A second headman was usually appointed to assist the first.[62]

On the other hand, the rewards brought by the Atlantic trade were not distributed equally. In the Sierra Leonean colony, the Kru chief headman received a relatively large pay in addition to the special gifts he received from each laborer he administered.[63] American traders who were actively involved with the Kru paid them as follows: "An unspecified period of service was fixed at twelve dollars for the head Kruman, ten dollars for the second head Kruman, and eight dollars for each of the members of the gang."[64]

This development was to have deepening effects on the political formation of the coastal Kru. Contrary to Professor S. Holsoe's argument that they looked at their newly acquired wealth only in terms of material wealth, the Kru, like the Vais, did indeed use their new wealth to capture political positions. A portion of the wealth accumulated was given in the form of gifts to the *pantonnyefue* or old people of the town for political favors.[65] In fact, those who worked on ships increasingly became the leading candidates for the office of *Krogba* or the "father of the town." Traditionally, the position was reserved for only elders. But as the Atlantic trade advanced to the pre-Liberian coast, so did the traditional rule change. A young man who had enough of the new wealth could now easily occupy the office.[66]

Like the Vais and Kru, the Atlantic trade affected the political formations of Glebo. By the beginning of the nineteenth century, the various subdivisions of the Glebo ethnic group had merged into a relatively large politicial confederation. Hence, the Council of the Confederation drafted a constitution for the Glebo people in 1822. King Freeman, who seems to have received his title from his trading contacts with the Europeans, became the leader of the Glebo in the 1830s and 1840s. He was later succeeded by a chief from Rocktown.[67] In fact, a number of Glebo coastal towns became powerful, both politically and economically because of the direct and indirect involvement of a large number of that ethnic group with the Atlantic trade.[68]

Another side product of European commercial involvement with the West African coast was the coming into being of a mulatto class. The members of this class were the offspring of the Europeans who traded on the coast and the African women with whom they came into contact. By the 1600s, there were already some successful mulattoes on the West African coast. The most prominent among them included the Cleveland Caulkers, the Abraham Tuckers, and the Charles Rogers.[69] Like the "assimilated" African chiefs and traders, these trading families did help to enhance the expansion of the Atlantic trade to the West African coast. They served, as Walter Rodney has observed, as "interpreters, and carried out all the tasks of middlemen in the coastal trade, from acting as pilots on the rivers to serving as commercial advisors to the local ruling class."[70] Some European merchants employed Peter Tucker, a descendant of the Tucker family, as an interpreter in Sierra Leone in 1684. One of the Rogers' family was offered a position as a sailor in 1688.[71]

The roles of the mulattoes were not only limited to insignificant positions. The English Royal African Company appointed two members of the Rogers family to administer its trading activities around the Cape Mount region.[72] This kind of role brought tremendous wealth and power to some mulattoes. The wealth and power of Henry Tucker, as described by the English trader Nicholas Owen, attests to this:

> He has been in England, Spain, Portugal, and is a master of the English tongue; he has six or seven wives and numerous offspring of sons and daughters; his strength consists of his own slaves and their children, who has built a town about him and serves as his gremetos on all occasions. This man bears the character of a fair trader among the Europeans, but to the contrary among the blacks. His riches set him above the kings and his numerous people above being surprised by war; almost all the blacks owe him money, which brings a dread of being stopt upon that account, so that he is esteemed and feared by all who have the misfortune to be in his power. He's a fat man and fair spoken, and lives after the manner of the English, having his house well furnish'd with English goods, and his table tolerably well

furnish'd with the country produce. He dressed gayley and commonly makes use of silver at his table, having a good side board of plate.[73]

Evidently the Atlantic trade largely enhanced accumulation of such new wealth.[74] The main source of Tucker's wealth came from his selling of thousands of his people to European slavers. He employed the "debt traps" approach to accomplish his objective. In other words, Tucker created conditions whereby many local Africans became indebted to him. But as his main goal was their enslavement, he made sure that he would not accept anything from them other than their persons.[75]

This description could well be applied to nearly all the successful mulattoes. James Cleveland, a mulatto from pre-Sierra Leone,[76] was said to credit any African chief who requested it. This was done under the pretext that the chief who accepted such a loan would provide him with slaves. The village of the indebted chief who failed to honor the terms of the loan would be burned and his people enslaved. Before 1826, the mulattoes had penetrated the *Poro*, a powerful secret society of the Mande-speaking people of the area in question. This was intended to ensure the continued supply of slaves from the region. At Cape Mount, the Rogers family and the Kru collaborated with Blanco, the Spanish slaver, to secure this objective.[77]

Evidently, the mulattoes did achieve a respectable social status on the West African coast. But one could reasonably agree with Rodney's statement that:

> Their political power, far from resting on a traditional kinship basis, could only have been achieved in spite of previous social proscription. . . . At every juncture, their rise to social and political prominence must be seen in relation to commerce with the Europeans. . . . They squeezed the Africans to make as much personal profit as possible, but essentially they served the wider interests of European commercial capitalism.[78]

It is not, therefore, surprising that the mulattoes, like the African traders who showed signs of being unwilling to collaborate with the

Europeans, were usually opposed. Walter Charles, a key English trader on the Grain Coast, declared in 1728 that: "I will take effectual care while I stay in the country that no white black man shall make figure here above what meanest natives do."[79] To accomplish this, Charles tried to influence the local chiefs around the Sherbro Island and the Cape Mount area to get rid of the mulattoes by telling them that the mulattoes "were treating the African masses tyrannically, and insulting their kings." The Portuguese also made a similar charge against the mulattoes who traded on the coast of Upper Guinea.[80]

Obviously, the European traders made the charges to ensure their commercial domination. Despite this attempt, there were some mulattoes and African chiefs who resisted. The resistors included Barnabe Lopeze, an Afro-Portuguesewho, together with his African supporters, succeeded in expelling the Royal African Company from the Sherbro in 1727. This could also be said about Chief Tomba of the Grain Coast. He violently protested against the transatlantic slave trade in 1720. African slavers and their European counterparts, however, captured and executed him.[81]

Evidently this kind of opposition did not arrest the European commercial domination. The failure to stop this domination was influenced by three crucial factors: first, resistance was not the general response to the European advance in West Africa. Most of the coastal chiefs and mulattoes collaborated with the Europeans to promote their narrow interests. Second, the combined internal and external force the few resistors protested against was superior militarily. Besides, the continued economic and political survival of the resistors, like the non-resistors, depended on their subordinate collaboration with the European traders. This seems to explain why most of the Grain Coast's chiefs and mulattoes who were actively involved with the Atlantic trade became nothing but puppets by the nineteenth century. This legacy was promoted in colonial Africa and later inherited by most independent African countries.[82]

The new social arrangements of the Grain Coast were also brought about by the increasing demand for the non-human resources of that region. As noted, such resources included ivory and camwood. The increasing demand for ivory, for example, led, to the calling into being of a group of professional elephant hunters. Unlike before, the members of this group began to arm themselves with "long Dan guns loaded with small iron rods."[83] Hence, by the nineteenth century, there were villages of professional elephant hunters on the West African coast. The objective of this was to ensure the continued supply of ivory to the European traders.[84] As discussed earlier, the new development was to reduce greatly the numbers of that animal. Elephants were almost completed eliminated at Cape Mount which had once been home to a large herd.

Like the demand for ivory, the one for camwood was to affect the social formations of the region under study. The very fact that cutting, "rough-hewing," and transporting the trees to the coast was labor intensive meant that a large number of Africans were needed to accomplish such tasks. Because of this, coastal chiefs were required to persuade their people to cooperate. The chiefs were sometimes under pressure themselves. The leaders of the Royal African Company warned the king of the Sherbro Island, for example, that if he failed to provide enough laborers, they would be forced to look elsewhere. With his increasing reliance on the transatlantic trade for his material status and political leverage, the king seems to have been forced into compliance.[85]

Besides, several coastal towns were called into being by the camwood "industry." Africans from the interior were increasingly attracted by the new "industry."[86] Presumably, these were among the first group of West Africans to carry European ideas to the interior.

The Atlantic trade brought about other side effects. The trade did, for instance, clearly articulate an economic concept that emphasized profit making as its ultimate objective. This was to undermine the economy of "gainless barter" that characterized most indigenous West African societies.[87] Even crops like rice, which was not traditionally sold capitalistically, was now sold for "gainful purposes" as the Atlantic trade advanced on the Grain Coast.[88]

The other side effect included the way in which trade was conducted. Although it is not certain when it was introduced in West Africa, Europeans, coastal chiefs, and the mulattoes accepted the "dash"[89] or special gift as a well accepted part of the Atlantic trade that tied the three groups together. "Dash" was usually requested by a coastal chief from a mulatto or a European trader for an additional privilege of trading in his area. It was usually in the form of rum, tobacco, fibered materials, and perhaps guns and gunpowder when the transaction involved slaves.[90] As the Atlantic trade became more profitable, European traders were eager to induce coastal chiefs by offering them "bigger dash" for more advantageous privileges. It must, however, be borne in mind that the "dash" offered was only a small fraction of the anticipated wealth that was to be acquired.[91]

Also associated with the Atlantic trade was the gross unfairness that characterized it. John Newton described how the trade was conducted in 1752:

> Africans were viewed as persons to be robbed with impunity. Every act was employed to deceive them, and the European traders who achieved most in this regard had more to boast of. No article was delivered without tampering--the alcohol was adulterated with water, false heads were placed in the keys that contained gunpowder, and lengths were cut from the middle of cloth where missing portions were not readily noted. . . .[92]

What lasting effect this kind of trading practice had on West Africa is indeed difficult to speculate. It has, however, been lately charged that some of the unethical business dealings that are prevalent in West Africa today could be traced back to the early European commercial involvement with that region.[93]

But one argument seems to be certain: that the new commercial system introduced to the West African coast starting in the 1400s benefited the region only narrowly. This was heightened by the fact that the European goods exchanged for African slaves, ivory, camwood, gold, beeswax and pepper, largely benefited only the new, small privileged coastal class. Added to this was the fact that goods received, unlike the ones exported, were mostly consumable or too destructive to have brought about any meaningful economic development to coastal West Africa.[94]

As has been illustrated throughout this chapter, the Grain Coast was never static. Both internal and external forces were acting upon it, thus reinforcing the changing processes. The Manes' invasions and the Europeans' increasing involvement with the region attest to this argument. These developments led to new ones. The new social stratifications brought almost simultaneously by the two forces gives evidence of the last argument.

Taking all these into consideration, one could reasonably agree with the late Professor Walter Rodney that "it is totally misleading to refer to African society at the end of the slave trade as traditional."[95] In other words, the political, economic, and other social institutions of coastal West Africa had already been modified and reoriented to serve the needs of the Atlantic trade before the advance of the ACS to that region during the 1820s. As will be illustrated in the succeeding chapters, it was this coastal West African reality and the various social values inherent in the ACS that fundamentally determined the new institutional formation of what became Liberia.

NOTES

Chapter II

[1]The term pre-Liberia is used in this work to denote the region of the West African Coast that became Liberia after 1822.

[2]Rodney, *A History of*, p. 47.

[3]*Ibid*., p. 48.

[4]John Barbot, *A Description of the Coasts of North and South Guinea* (London, 1796), p. 96.

[5]William E. Welmers, "The Mande Languages," *Georgetown University Monograph Series*, No. 11 (1958), pp. 9-24.

[6]Fyfe, "Peoples of the Windward Coast," p. 159.

[7]Svend E. Holsoe, "Economic Activities in the Liberian Area: The Pre-European Period to 1900" in *Liberian Studies Series*, No. 6 (1979), p. 66.

[8]Rodney, *A History of*, p. 49.

[9]Malcolm Cowley, ed. *Adventures of an African Slaver: Being a True Account of the Life of Captain Theodore Canot* (Cleveland, 1942), p. 306. See also Christopher Fyfe, *Sierra Leone Inheritance (London*, 1964).

[10]Walter Rodney, "A Reconsideration of the Mane Invasion of Sierra Leone," *Journal of African History*, VIII (1967), p. 144.

[11]Ronald W. Davis, *Ethnohistorical Studies on the Kru Coast* (Newark, 1976), pp. 22-23.

[12]Christian P. Potholm, *The Theory and Practice of African Politics* (Englewood cliffs, 1979), p. 14.

[13]Davis, *Ethnohistorical Studies*, p. 25.

[14]*Ibid.*, p. 17.

[15]For the different views on this argument see Rodney's "Reconsideration of the Mane Invasion"; Peter Kreps, *Sierra Leone, 1400-1787* (Cambridge, 1967); Welmer's "The Mande Languages"; Svend Holsoe, "The Cassava-Leaf People: An Ethnohistorical Study of the Vai People with a Particular Emphasis on the Tewo Chiefdom." (Ph.D. Dissertation, Boston University, 1967).

[16]Cited in Holsoe, "Economic Activities," pp. 73-74.

[17]See the following works: Ronald Davis, "Historical Outline of the Kru Coast, Liberia, 1500 to the Present," (Ph.D. Dissertation, Indiana University, 1968). Merran Fraenkel, "Social Change on the Kru Coast of Liberia," *Africa*, XXXVI (1966); Rodney, *A History of*.

[18]Davis, *Ethnohistorical Studies*, p. 37.

[19]This has been discussed in detail in I. K. Sundiata, *Black Scandal: America and the Liberian Labor Crisis, 1929-1936* (Philidelphia, 1980).

[20]Thomas Ludlam, "An Account of the Kroomen on the Coast of Africa," *African Repository* I (1825), pp. 43-44. Ludlam, who arrived in West Africa in 1797, served as Governor of Sierra Leone. This article was published after his death. Kru trading activities during this period are also described in Joseph Corry, *Observations Upon the Windward Coast of Africa: The Religion, Character, Customs of the Natives* (London, 1807), pp. 53-54.

[21]George E. Brooks, *Yankee Traders: Old Coasters and African Middlemen: A History of American Legitimate Trade with West Africa in the Nineteenth Century* (Boston, 1970), pp. 322-323.

[22]Jane J. Martin, "The Dual Legacy: Government Authority and Mission Influence Among the Glebo of Eastern Liberia, 1834-1910," (Ph. D. Dissertation, Boston University, 1968), pp. 8-22; Rodney, "A Reconsideration of the Mane Invasion," pp. 219-246; Yves Person, "Des Kru en Haute-Volta," *Bulletin de l'Institute Francais de Afrique Noire*, XXVIII (1966), p. 491.

[23]Joseph Greenberg, *The Languages of Afica* (Bloomington, 1964), p. 39.

[24]Martin, "The Dual Legacy," p. 48.

[25]Gordon M. Haliburton, "Prophet Harris and His Works in Ivory Coast and Western Ghana," (Ph. D. Dissertation, University of London, 1967), p. 99.

[26]Martin, "The Dual Legacy," p. 49.

[27]C. R. Boxer, *Four Centuries of Portuguese Expansion, 1415-1825* (Los Angeles, 1969), p. 5.

[28]Rodney, *History of*, p. 71.

[29]*Ibid.* This was the name given to the pre-Liberian coast by the early European traders because of the abundance of grains they saw in the region.

[30]Carlo M. Cipolla, *Guns, Sails, and Empire: Technological Innovation and the Early Phases of European Expansion, 1400-1700* (New York, 1965), p. 135.

[31]Fyfe, "Peoples of the Windward Coast," p. 160.

[32]Rodney, *A History of*, p. 121; Holsoe, "Economic Acitvities in the Liberian Area," pp. 71-73.

[33]Rodney, *A History of*, pp. 126-127.

[34]Fyfe, "Peoples of the Windward Coast," p. 151.

[35]Fyfe, *Sierra Leone Inheritance*, pp. 50-62.

[36]Rodney, *A History of*, p. 127.

[37]*Ibid.*, p. 153.

[38]For the increasing British involvement with the Gambian gold trade, see John Gray, *History of the Gambia* (London, 1940).

[39]Rodney, *A History of*, p. 154.

[40]Quoted in *Ibid.*, p. 155.

[41]Barbot, *A Description of*, p. 106; Fyfe, "The Peoples of the Windward Coast," p. 157.

[42]Rodney, *A History of*, p. 160.

[43]*Ibid.*, pp. 158-160.

[44]See the following works about this argument: Philip Curtin, *The Atlantic Slave Trade: A Census* (Madison, 1969); Eric Williams, *Capitalism and Slavery* (Chapel Hill, 1944); Marcus W. Jernegan, *Laboring and Dependent Classes in Colonial America, 1607-1783* (Chicago, 1931); Richard Dunn, *Sugar and Slaves: The Rise of the Planter Class in the English West Indies. 1624-1713* (New York, 1971); and Gary Nash, *Red, White, and Black: The Peoples of Early America* (Englewood Cliffs, 1974).

[45]Daniel P. Mannix and Malcolm Cowley, *Black Cargoes: A History of the Atlantic Slave Trade, 1518-1865* (New York, 1962), p. 106.

[46]*Ibid.*, p. 3.

[47]Christopher Fyfe, "The Dynamics of African Dispersal: The Transatlantic Slave Trade," in Martin L. Kilson and Robert Rotberg, eds., *The African Diaspora: Interpretive Essays* (Cambridge, 1976), pp. 57-74. Also see Leslie B. Route, "The African in Colonial Brazil," and Paul Edwards and James Walvin, "Africans in Britain, 1500-1800," in the same volume.

[48]Mannix and Cowley, *Black Cargoes*, p. 3.

[49]Rodney, *A History of*, p. 97.

[50]*Ibid.*, p. 102.

[51]*Ibid.*, p. 103.

[52]This is another name given by historians to the coastal area of Liberia and the Ivory Coast.

[53]Davis, *Ethnohistorical Studies*, p. 33.

[54]Fyfe, "Peoples of the Windward Coast," p. 156.

[55]Rodney, *A History of*, pp. 77-80, 202-205.

[56]Curtin, *The Atlantic Slave Trade*, pp. 128, 150. See especially tables 33, 34, 65, 67, and 77.

[57]Rodney, *A History of*, p. 253; John Atkins, *A Voyage to Guinea, Brazil and the West Indies* (London, 1775), p. 73; Cowley, ed., *Adventures of* p. 302.

[58]Davis, *Ethnohistorical Studies*, pp. 34-35.

[59]*African Repository*, XIV (1840), p. 293.

[60]*Ibid.*, XXIV (1848), pp. 283-284.

[61]John L. Wilson, *Western Africa: Its History, Conditions and Prospects* (New York, 1856), pp. 106-108; Ludlum, "An Account of," p. 46.

[62]Christopher Fyfe, *A History of Sierra Leone* (London, 1962), p. 135; Mary Kingsley, *Travels in West Africa* (London, 1897), pp. 644-655; Raymond L. Buell, *The Native Problem in Africa*, Vol. II (New York, 1928), pp. 774-781.

[63]Davis, *Ethnohistorical Studies*, p. 39.

[64]*Ibid.*

[65]*Ibid.* For Holsoe's argument on this, see his "Economic Activities in the Liberian Area," especially pp. 71-72.

[66]Davis, *Ethnohistorical Studies*, p. 39.

[67]Martin, "The Dual Legacy," p. 22.

[68]J. D. Fage, *A History of Africa* (New York, 1978), p. 247.

[69]Rodney, *A History of*, p. 216.

[70]*Ibid.*, p. 203.

[71]*Ibid.*, p. 217.

[72]*Ibid.*

[73]E. Martin, ed., Nicholas Owen, *Journal of a Slave Dealer on the Coast of Africa and America from 1746 to Year 1757* (London, 1930), p. 76.

[74]Rodney, *A History of*, p. 218.

[75]*Ibid.*, pp. 217-218.

[76]Claude George, *The Rise of British West Africa* (London, 1903), pp. 65-67.

[77]Canot, *Adventures of*, p. 300.

[78]Rodney, *A History of*, pp. 220-222.

[79]*Ibid*., p. 213.

[80]*Ibid*.

[81]Atkins, *Voyage to Guinea*, pp. 42, 72.

[82]Mittleman, *Underdevelopment and Transition*, pp. 9-10; F. H. Cardoso and E. Faletto, *Dependency and Development in Latin America* (Los Angeles, 1979), p. xvi; F. Mansour, "Third World Revolt and Self Reliant Auto-Center Strategy of Development," in Kim Q. Hill, ed., *Towards a New Strategy for Development* (New York, 1978), pp. 203-206.

[83]Phillip Beaver, *African Memoranda Relative to an Attempt to Establish a British Settlement on the Island of Bolama in the Year 1792* (London, 1805), pp. 318-319.

[84]Barbot, *A Description of*, p. 109.

[85]Rodney, *History of*, p. 160.

[86]A. G. Laing, *Travels in the Timannee Koronka and Soolima countries* (London, 1825), p. 78.

[87]Karl Polanyi, "Sortings and Ounce Trade in the West African Slave Trade," *Journal of African History*, V (1961), pp. 381-393.

[88]The Loma, Gola, and the Kpelle ethnic groups of Liberia continue to admit that rice was not traditionally allowed to be sold for profit.

[89]"Dash" is still used in Liberia as a kind of "bribery" to gain political positions or business privileges. It has long been alleged that

local and foreign businessmen employ the practice to promote their interests; and so do giant companies like the Firestone Rubber Company and all major iron working companies in Liberia.

[90]Rodney, *A History of*, p. 176.

[91]This seems to be a logical nature of capitalist transaction. For a detailed analysis of this argument, see Ernest Mandel, *Late Capitalism* (London, 1975), pp. 343-377.

[92]B. Martin and M. Superrell, eds., John Newton, "Thoughts Upon the African Trade, 1750-54," *Journal of a Slave Trader* (London, 1962), p. 81.

[93]Former President Alhaji S. Shagari of Nigeria made this charge to American television audiences during his visit to America in 1979. See also note 89.

[94]Fyfe, "The Peoples of the Windward Coast," p. 160.

[95]Rodney, *A History of*, p. 259.

CHAPTER III

ESTABLISHMENT OF THE COLONY AND THE AFRICANS' RESPONSE

The advance of the ACS on the pre-Liberian coast during the early 1800s precipitated reactions from the Africans of that region. Their reactions were to bring about counterresponses from the ACS. These developments, which were occasionally carried out violently, had to do directly with the questions of land ownership and the attempt on the part of American settlers to replace the coastal Africans. The emerging tension was also aggravated by the dissimilarities of the social values of the ACS and those of the Africans.

As already noted, the main objective of the ACS was to colonize the emancipated black Americans somewhere outside America. Although some colonizationists had suggested Latin America and other places, it was finally agreed that West Africa would be the best alternative. The preference for West Africa was influenced by the following factors: the British already had a colony there;[1] Paul Cuffe, a successful black American merchant from Boston, had established a trading contact on the West Coast in the early nineteenth century. Although he did not live long enough to develop fully his venture, his experiment illustrated that black colonization in that region was possible.[2] Besides it was reasoned that if the blacks were colonized in West Africa, it would dismiss the abolitionists' allegation that the desire of the ACS was to deport free blacks to an unfamiliar land. This reasoning was influenced by the fact that the ancestral background of the blacks brought to America could be traced to Africa.[3]

It was against this background that Reverend Samuel J. Mills of Connecticut was appointed by the ACS, in November 1817, to travel to West Africa to locate a suitable site for the proposed colony.[4] The

ACS also instructed that Mills be accompanied by Ebenezer Burgess, a lecturer in mathematics from New England.[5] The two men were ordered to go to West Africa by way of England. In England, they were to consult the president of the African Institution, and humanitarians such as W. Wilberforce, J. Butterworth, J. Stephen, W. Allen, W. Vaughan, J. Reyner, S. Cock, and J. Roberts. Besides, they were to meet Earl H. Bathurst, who headed the British Colonial Office, to discuss issues that were relevant to their African mission.[6]

Their next tasks were to travel to West Africa where they were to meet with the British colonial administration of Sierra Leone. Following this, the two men were to study thoroughly the coastal area between Sierra Leone and the Sherbro Island, including the climatic conditions, the land, and different ethnic groups, the rivers and mountains, and the possibility of agricultural development. They were told to focus their main attention on the Sherbro Island, the site of the proposed colony (see map p. 104). Further, they were to document "accurate accounts" of the areas already claimed by Europeans and those under African control.[7]

With these instructions, the two men sailed to London on the ship *Electra* in November, 1817. In London, they were well received, and so was the main objective of their mission.[8] The cordial reception given to the two Americans was influenced by the fact that the objective of their mission was similar to what the British had already achieved in West Africa. Sierra Leone colony, established by the British on the West African coast in 1787 as a home for their "poor blacks" from England and emancipated slaves from Nova Scotia and Jamaica, provided a parallel to the proposed American colony.[9]

With the support of British colonial office officials and humanitarians, both Mills and Burgess now sailed to West Africa. By March 13, 1818, they had reached the Gambian coast, where they saw a few European missionaries converting the coastal Gambians to Christianity. Their attention was captured by the treeless plain of the region.[10]

By March 20, the two Americans had sailed to Sierra Leone where Mills declared that:

> The altars on these mountains which the natives had dedicated to the devils, are falling before the temples of the living God, like the image of Dagon before the ark. The time is coming when the dwellers in these villages and on these mountains will sing hosannahs to the Son of David. Distant tribes will learn their song. Ethiopia will stretch forth her hands unto God and Worship.[11]

Upon arrival, both Mills and Burgess dicided to meet with the British administrators of Sierra Leone. They first attempted to present a letter, given to them in London by Earl Bathurst, to Governor Sir Charles MaCarthy. The letter outlined the objectives of the ACS and requested the Sierra Leonean authorities to cooperate with the two ACS' representatives in their pursuit. Because Governor MaCarthy was not in the colony, the letter was given to the Chief Justice, E. Fitzgerald. The very fact that the two Americans were courteously received and their objectives well sanctioned by the British colonial administrators of Sierra Leone seem to suggest that the Secretary of State for the Colonies might have strongly recommended the colonization scheme of the ACS.

It must be pointed out, however, that there was opposition to the increasing advance of the ACS on the coast of West Africa even at this stage. The opposition came from British merchants who were stationed in Sierra Leone. They feared that if an American colony was established in the vicinity of Sierra Leone, their commercial interests would be undermined.[12]

Despite this opposition, British colonial leaders were not ready at this time to give in to the British merchants in Sierra Leone. This seems to have been influenced by the fact that wealth accumulated through commerce by the foregoing trading groups was not yet great enough to determine British colonial policies in West Afica.[13] Further, the lobbies of British humanitarians and evangelists on behalf of the ACS were too influential to have been easily undermined.[14] But as will be illustrated in subsequent chapters, British support for the ACS was not to continue, especially after the 1840s.

It was against this background, that the two Americans continued to be well received in Sierra Leone. During their stay in that colony, they were introduced to prominent members of the Friendly Society (FS), a West African coastal Creole fraternal organization that was started by Cuffe. One of its influential members, John Kizell, was asked to assist the ACS' representatives, a request Kizell accepted delightfully, but also cautiously.[15]

Kizell's social background influenced his response to this request. Kizell was a son of an African chief. While he was visiting his uncle on the coast, he was kidnapped and sold to European slavers at a place called Gallinas. From Gallinas, Kizell was sent to Charleston, South Carolina, where he was resold.[16] Kizell was brought to Charleston just before the American Revolutionary War started. A few years after his arrival, Sir Henry Clinton, a British colonial general, took the city. As part of the British strategy to undermine the American rebels, the British issued a special proclamation which maintained that slaves who would join them against the Americans would be immediately set free.[17]

Kizell was among the slaves who took advantage of the proclamation. He quickly became a British loyalist, and he, in fact, fought under the command of Colonel Patrick Ferguson. It is argued that he was present when the latter was killed near King's Mountain in North Carolina on October 7, 1780.[18] The British honored the terms by which Kizell had joined them as the war came to an end. He was set free and sent to Nova Scotia, later to England, and finally, in 1792, to Sierra Leone.[19]

As a westernized African, Kizell was employed by the British to promote his newly acquired values in Africa, and he thus became a member of what would be the new emerging coastal commercial class. In 1810, the new British Governor of Sierra Leone, Columbine, sent Kizell to his people on the Sherbro Island with the following messages:

> I have sent Mr. Kizell to visit you on my part in order that you may communicate to him anything that you may wish to say to me. . . . I hope you will allow my friend, Mr. Kizell,

to have sufficient portion of ground or territory for him to build a town, and to point out to you the proper mode of rearing those articles of trade which will supply you with European commodities. You cannot have the least reason to be jealous of him; he is one of yourselves; and he has the welfare of you and your country earnestly at heart; and I entreat you to forward his views as much as possible, and to join him in noble endeavour to make yourselves and your children great and your country happy. I shall leave the transaction entirely to yourselves as I do not intend to send a single European to live at Kizelltown; but I shall furnish . . . tools for cultivation.[20]

The above description of Kizell left out other things. As noted, Kizell was a member of the emerging coastal commercial class. He owned about six hundred acres of land at a place that was not far from Sherbro Island. He bought the land from King Fora and his headman Rango in 1814 for the sum of $150.[21] Indeed, Kizell was an influential figure on the coastal area between Sierra Leone and pre-Liberia. His main source of influence lay in his successful manipulation of the Atlantic trade and values brought by the trade. This demanded his continued cooperation with the Europeans who determined the trade. Little wonder Kizell liked the mediating role assigned to him by the British.

It could thus be argued that Kizell was both skillful and tactful in his new role. During their travel from Sierra Leone to the Sherbro Island, Kizell responded to every question asked by his American guests in the way that he anticipated would be most pleasing to them. When he was informed about the main objective of the ACS, his reaction, for example, was that the colonization scheme "had its origin in heaven."[22] Kizell sounded like later Pan-Africanists when he declared on April 14, 1818 that:

> Africa belongs to Africans abroad as well as those now in the country; and if they are disposed to return, land they must and shall have. They have not forfeited a right to the inheritance of their fathers by being carried by force from their country.[23]

Despite this Pan-Africanist sentiment, the emphasis was mainly designed to correspond with the ACS' rationale that the desire to colonize free blacks to West Africa was a moral undertaking.[24]

Although he told his American guests what accorded with the main objective of the ACS, Kizell did not allow them to have a direct access to his African power base. The area that he recommended for the colonization scheme was, for example, some several miles from Campelar, the place where he owned a vast amount of land.[25] Hence, just before they arrived at the Sherbro Island, Kizell told his American guests that it would well serve the objective of the mission if he conversed with the leaders of that island without their presence. With little choice, the two Americans decided to accept, though reluctantly, the above suggestion. Following this, Kizell, together with his African assistants, now sailed to the Sherbro to meet with the leaders of that place.[26]

The aim of Kizell's behavior was to protect his role as a mediator between the non-or "semi-assimilated"[27] coastal Africans and European traders. Like most members of the coastal elites, Kizell was aware of the fact that if the Europeans and later the Americans succeeded in establishing direct contact with those Africans, he would not be needed as a mediator. Of course, this would have done away with one of his main sources of income and power. This seems to explain why the members of the new coastal elite made sure to impress their people, the Europeans, and later the American settlers, that they were indispensable. They did this by trying to please all the foregoing groups. Nearly all the most successful elites who conducted trade along the coastal area between Sierra Leone and pre-Liberia gave, for instance, the pleasing illusion to both Mills and Burgess that land for the colonization scheme could be obtained easily. In fact, Mills and Burgess left the area with the misleading view that they had been offered lands for the colonization initiative by such successful coastal African traders as Thomas Caulker, John Tucker, and Chiefs Fara, Yaltucker, and Pa Poosoo.[28] Kizell had earlier given the impression to the two Americans that Chief Couber of the Sherbro Island was receptive to almost every design of the ACS.[29]

As suggested, the elites also tactfully created a condition whereby their people came to view them as indispensable. The method employed in doing this was similar to the one used in impressing the Europeans and the Americans. This was illustrated when Kizell told Chief Couber that:

> Two gentlemen . . . have come . . . from America, the city of Washington. . . . They have sent to see King Sherbro, and to obtain a place for some black people who are freed in that country, and will come to set down by King Sherbro, if he will give some ground where they may settle. . . . If he gives them a place, it will be a great advantage to his children and people; for these people will bring the arts and knowledge of cultivation, and will establish schools.[30]

With this kind of benevolent characterization of the objective of the ACS, Chief Couber became increasingly receptive to the idea of that movement, though he refused to offer land for the scheme on the ground that all the other leaders were not present.[31] Despite this setback, Kizell accomplished his ultimate objective. While the Africans viewed him as their spokesman, his American guests reasoned that he was indispensable to their mission. In fact, both parties hailed Kizell as the most respectful man in the Sherbro and Cape Mount regions. Mills was to give this euphoric description of Kizell:

> Mr. Kizell is a second Paul Cuffee. He has a good mind and considerable knowledge. His writings discover him to be a man of sense and worth. He has a good heart, and no one can be more anxious for the temporal and spiritual welfare of the Africans, and their descendants. He has enlarged views, believes with the fullest confidence, thinks the time has arrived when the descendants of Africa abroad shall begin to return to their own country. His mind relies on the promises of God. Ethiopia shall soon stretch forth her hands unto God.[32]

This description failed to take into consideration the underlying force that determined Kizell's reaction to the ACS. His desire to accumulate additional wealth, not humanitarian or religious impulses as the quotation implied, fundamentally shaped his reaction. His benevolent emphasis was mainly designed to facilitate the achievement of this goal. As will be illustrated, the successors of Mills and Burgess were to learn of this in the 1820s.

Like the roles of the westernized Africans on the West African coast, those of Mills, Burgess, and their successors were, indeed, determined by various social values. The values which prevailed among leaders and supporters of the ACS deeply influenced the perception of Mills and Burgess on the West African coast. This was especially the case for the former. In Gambia, the British "westernization" of that colony greatly moved Mills. He was mainly captured by the architectural structures of the colonial buildings and the newly organized African army. He was to describe the latter as "above the ordinary status, well formed, and neatly dressed." He later added that the westernized African soldiers "appeared to be quite expert and intelligent."[33] In Sierra Leone, the school established by the British profoundly impressed Mills. This mood was spelled out thus:

> In March 1818 we visited schools in Freetown. In the male school were about 200 neat, active, and intelligent boys, divided into eight classes, under the superintendance of Mr. Horton whose perseverance and fidelity are entitled to high commendation. We saw the writings of the boys, and heard them read and spell. In the female school were about 100 little girls, many of whom could read and sew. These schools would do no dishonour to an English or American village. . . .[34]

Mills' appreciation did not, however, extend to those African values that were not westernized. He described African music, for example, as "dull and monotonous."[35] He later referred to the African villages he visited as places of darkness. Of course, this characterization of coastal West Africa was among the ACS' rationalizations for bringing the "sun of righteousness" to that region.[36] Mills contradicted earlier and late pro-slavery thinkers when he derogatorily argued that "slave traders have made even savages more vicious. The people are generally idle, superstitious, self-indulgent and fond of ardent spirits."[37] The paternalistic attribute of the ACS was reemphasized when Mills described the non-westernized Africans as people who were "only children of a larger growth, and would hope by a temporary conformity, gradually to wean them from their vicious customs."[38]

The failure of the early ACS' representatives to appreciate anything African was to force them to rely heavily on only those things and Africans they considered westernized. But this attitude would long persist and it was to slow down the advance of the ACS on the West African coast. To understand this, it is necessary to examine the advance and the counterreactions to it after 1821.

Although Mills died from malaria on June 16, 1818, his reports on the West African coast were sent to the ACS in Washington. The reports gave the illusion that the objective of his mission to Africa had worked out as planned by the ACS. In his reports, for instance, Mills maintained that lands had already been obtained for the colonization scheme. This report was based on the flattering gestures of Caulker, Tucker, Fora, Yaltucker, and Pa Poosoo, who were all successful traders on the coast. As discussed before, the gestures were mainly designed to protect the mediatory role of these traders. They could not possibly allow their role to be undermined since it was bringing them tremendous wealth and power.

But because Mills and Burgess held high admiration for everything western, they were bound to accept at face value every action of the Africans they considered westernized. This explains why they uncritically accepted the gestures of Kizell and other coastal elites like him. As will be noted, this attitude toward the westernized Africans was not, however, to continue. This change came about when the advance of the ACS began to conflict radically with the interest of the elites.

The reports provided by Mills had an enormous impact on the ACS' initial effort to establish a colony on the West African coast. The reports heavily influenced the unanimous decision of the ACS' leadership to initiate a colony.

It was against this background that the organization chartered a ship named the *Elizabeth* to transport eighty-eight free black Americans to West Africa. The voyage actually began at the port of New York on

January 31, 1820. The immigrants were either newly emancipated or blacks who had been freed long before. They came mainly from Virginia, Maryland, the District of Columbia, Pennsylvania, and New York. More than half of the group was composed of women and children. Nearly all the immigrants were deeply religious. Of course, this was one of the requirements for those who wanted to sail to the proposed colony. The group was headed by the following three whites: Samuel Bacon, John Bankson, and Samuel Crozer. Crozer served as chief representative of the ACS. Bacon represented the United States government. He was assisted by Bankson.[39]

On March 9, the *Elizabeth* anchored at Freetown, the chief seaport of Sierra Leone. In Freetown, Governor MaCarthy received the new arrivals. Following this, they now proceeded to Sherbro Island, the place designated for the proposed settlement by the ACS. But the misleading information provided by Mills increasingly became an obstacle to progress. Kizell, who Mills had said would be present to receive the new arrivals, was nowhere to be found. Added to this was the failure of the U. S. Navy to keep its promise of making some basic preparations at the Sherbro before the arrival of the Americans.[40] With these problems, Bacon, who was to be the chief administrator of the arriving settlers, decided to purchase a boat to transfer goods from the *Elizabeth* to the Sherbro and to try to locate Kizell. The purchase of a boat was a necessity, since the *Elizabeth* was too large to sail closer to the Sherbro or other similar locations.[41]

Having accomplished this, Bacon arrived on March 20, 1820 at Campelar, the "estate" of Kizell. Bacon received a friendly welcome. He testified: "I was well received with joy by Mr. Kizell and his people. We wept as we walked together to his house. I dined with him on fish and rice, dressed with palm oil. . . . Mr. Kizell is a pious man."[42]

But despite this hospitable gesture, Kizell's reaction to the advance of the ACS became intensely resentful. This was illustrated when a group of chiefs around the Sherbro area were called to discuss the main purpose of Bacon's mission. At that gathering, Kizell, who served as the chief mediator between Bacon and the chiefs, intentionally downplayed almost every discussion that might have helped to facilitate the realization of the objective of the ACS. This attitude was reinforced when a large amount of goods of the arriving settlers was brought to Kizell's "estate."[43] Presumably, Kizell felt threatened by the potential advance of the ACS. Kizell's growing hostility threatened to cause difficulty for the colonization initiative.

As this development became clear, Bacon decided to pursue an alternative. Accordingly, he decided to communicate directly with Chief Couber of the Sherbro Island. But this move only intensified Kizell's suspicion that the ACS was trying to penetrate his social base of power.[44] No wonder Kizell's resentful attitude toward the ACS was reinforced. This was shown when Kizell began openly to incite the Africans to turn against the colonization scheme. This strategy worked; Bacon was unable to convince the chiefs to provide land for the colonization initiative. The ACS was thus forced to admit that Kizell was responsible for its first major failure in Africa.[45]

But there was one other cause for the failure. The mortality rate was high among the Americans sent to West Africa.[46] Mills, who made the unwise recommendation to the ACS, died from malaria as he returned to America in June of 1818. Most of the white administrators who succeeded him were to meet a similar fate. Bacon died of fever on May 2, 1820, and Bankson met the same calamity on May 13. Crozer had died earlier.[47] Twenty-five of the arriving black settlers also died of fever or malaria.[48]

Because of the death of all the white leaders, a new power arrangement was made. The authority to administer the American immigrants on the Sherbro Island was entrusted to Reverend Daniel Coker, a capable black Methodist Episcopalian preacher. But Coker was to face some of the same problems his predecessors had earlier confronted. In addition to the increasing death rate among the immigrants, there was also a shortage of basic necessities. The net result of this was the decline in morale and discipline among the settlers.

As a result, militant opposition to Coker emerged. Some of the black settlers openly declared, for instance, that they would not recognize Coker's authority. This was a result of the allegation that Coker had earlier appeased the white administrators at the expense of the blacks.[49] It was because of these developments that Coker and the settlers he administered decided to make a tactical retreat to Sierra Leone, where they were given refuge at Fourah Bay, near Freetown.[50] Therefore, the attempt to establish an American settlement on the Sherbro Island did not materialize.

This did not mean, however, that the ACS' initiative was all over. The society, as a continuation of its colonization initiative, sent another group of settlers to the West African coast on the ship *Nautilus* one year after the retreat. The *Nautilus* anchored at Sierra Leone on March 9, 1821. The new arrivals were headed by Jonathan B. Winn and Ephrain Bacon, who represented the U. S. government and by Joseph Andrus and Christain Wiltberger, who represented the ACS.[51]

Following their temporary stay at Fourah Bay, the new arrivals, together with some of the earlier settlers, now sailed toward the Sherbro. The Sherbro Island was not, however, their main destination. In fact, the ACS had warned them not to establish a permanent settlement on that island. Of course, this decision was arrived at because of the unhealthy conditions and the obstacles posed by Kizell and the other leaders of that place.

As a result of these factors, the Americans were forced to direct their attention to the coastal region that became Liberia. Hence, on March 27, 1821, they arrived at Cape Mount where they met a mulatto slaver named John Mills and his assistant who was a "semi-assimilated" African. The former aptly told the Americans about the fertileness of Cape Montserrado, the place that actually became the starting base of Liberia. This gesture on the part of J. Mills seems to have been designed to discourage the Americans from establishing a settlement near his trading outposts as they would have undermined his transactions in human beings.[52]

In any case, the Americans were motivated by this piece of information and began to sail enthusiastically toward Cape Montserrado. Shortly after their departure from Cape Mount, they arrived at Cape Montserrado, where they called upon King Peter, a powerful coastal trader of that region (see map p. 104). Like Kizell and the other coastal elites, King Peter responded to the call in a cautious and tactical manner. Being aware of their objective, King Peter sent a message to the Americans informing them that he would not accept their gifts nor approve their colonization scheme.[53]

King Peter's reaction was mainly influenced by his desire to protect his involvement with the slave trade. While the *Nautilus* was at anchor at Cape Montserrado, a ship flying the French flag was waiting nearby for newly captured slaves.[54] No wonder King Peter declined to meet with the Americans, for among the objectives of their mission were the establishment of a permanent settlement and abolition of the slave trade in the region in question. For King Peter, the wealth and power that the Atlantic slave trade was bringing to him were too significant to have been easily replaced by an uncertain alternative. But who would reasonably argue that King Peter was any less altruistic than those prominent members of the ACS who sanctioned slavery in America but were attempting to stop it some five thousand miles away?[55]

The unyielding response to the request of the Americans did not, however, cause them to abandon their search for a suitable site for a settlement. In fact, by April 2, the American representatives had sailed to Grand Bassa, a place several miles southeast of Montserrado. There, some Africans came to trade, bringing with them trading goods such as "fowls, fish, oysters, palm oil, cassava, yams, plantains, bananas, limes, pineapple and pine wine" which they wanted to barter for "tobacco, pipes, and beads."[56]

During the transaction, the Americans were able to meet with one Jack Ben, another prominent trader. The Americans presented special "dashes" of one gun, some gunpowder, tobacco, pipes, and beads to Ben. Although these "gifts" were accepted, they were received with reservation. Indeed, following the offer, Ben immediately requested the Americans to state their objective. As might have been expected, the reaction of the Americans was that they needed land for a permanent settlement. With this spelled out, Ben became intensely curious about the wisdom of having accepted the "gifts." His concern was reinforced when the Americans told him that if land was provided, and a settlement established they would:

> . . . make a town where ships would come and trade with cloths, guns, beads, knives, tobacco, and pipes, and take in

> return their ivory, palm oil, rice, and everything they grew in the field; that they would not then need to sell any more people, but might learn to cultivate the ground, and make other things to sell for whatever they wanted.[57]

It was not, therefore, amazing that Ben became increasingly distrustful of the Americans, for his tie with the Atlantic slavetrade was rewarding. This explains why he committed himself only vaguely and reluctantly to the idea of establishing a colony in his area.

But the Americans interpreted this gesture on the part of Ben paternalistically. This was shown by their reaction that "it indeed requires much patience to deal with these children of the forest."[58] As noted before, this kind of description was among the concepts most of the early prominent members of the ACS held of the Africans and their descendants in the New World. It was, therefore, not surprising that the people they sent to Africa were to articulate similar views.[59]

Having failed to understand why King Peter and Ben acted as they did, the Americans now decided to return to Sierra Leone with only ambiguous promises from the two men. Added to this was their declining health. Indeed, Andrus died on July 28, 1821, and Winn and his wife were to follow suit. In fact, E. Bacon, the brother of the late S. Bacon, and his wife were among the few white survivors among the second group sent to Africa. They managed to return to the United States by way of Barbados.[60]

Despite this second setback, the attempt to establish a colony on the West African coast went forward. In fact, in 1821, the ACS decided to send another group of immigrants to West Africa on the ship *Alligator*. The third group included four whites and thirty-five blacks. Dr. Eli Ayres, a white physician from Baltimore, headed the new arrivals.[61]

Later, an American naval schooner which was commanded by one Robert Stockton arrived to assist the new arrivals. On December 12, 1821, Dr. Ayres sailed with Stockton to Cape Montserrado, the most hopeful place for the anticipated settlement. Following their arrival at

Cape Montserrado, the two men decided to call upon King Peter who had earlier been contacted by Dr. Ayres' predecessors. As before, the ACS requested King Peter to provide land for the proposed colony. The Americans decided to offer King Peter "gifts," such as rum, tobacco, and cloth. Seemingly, these "gifts" were offered to induce the King to cooperate; however, this attempt did not work. In fact, the King's reaction was that he would not sell Cape Montserrado to the Americans because "his women would cry aplenty." He decided, nevertheless, to appease the Americans by telling them that he would meet with them the next day.[62]

But at this critical juncture, the patience of the Americans was running out. They reasoned that only through superior pressure would the King and his people come to terms with them. This, coupled with the refusal of King Peter to meet with the Americans, caused the latter to decide that an aggressive measure should be taken. It was against this background that Dr. Ayres and Stockton decided to travel to King Peter's village, a place some six miles from the coast. The two men reached the village on December 15, 1821. But the arrival of the Americans only reinforced the suspicion and the displeasure of the King and his people. This was clearly spelled out when the King angrily asked Dr. Ayres and Stockton "what do you want the land for?"[63] He also accused the Americans of trying to bring about war and stop the trade in human beings.[64]

The inhospitable response to the Americans, on the other hand, only reinforced the view already held by them that only through their guns could the King and his people be forced into compliance. This iron-hand approach was carried out, and its result realized, as the Americans had anticipated. The whole event was later dramatized by Richard West in this way:

> Stockton pulled out his pistol, cocked it and gave it to Ayres with the instruction to shoot if necessary. He then aimed another at King Peter's head. Having thus ensured an attentive audience, he lectured the company on the advantages of a settlement.[65]

With this pressure, the Americans forced King Peter and five other important leaders of the region to yield to their demands. On December 15, 1821, Cape Montserrado was allegedly bartered for the following items: "guns, gunpowder, beads, cloths, mirrors, food, and tobacco," the net value of which was less than $300.[66]

Although it was seen as a victory over "barbarianism" by the Americans, the transaction actually reinforced the emerging tension between the two groups. It was further intensified by an event that occurred at the beginning of 1822. Early in that year, a British ship that was carrying some recaptives to Sierra Leone wrecked just near the coast of Montserrado. As was always the practice on the coast, some Africans who lived not too far from the Cape looted the wrecked ship. This action on the part of the Africans precipitated an immediate reaction from the Americans who were just arriving at the newly "purchased" Cape. Being threatened by the looting, the Americans decided to open fire on the looters. Ironically, flames from the guns of the Americans set fire to their newly built warehouse, thus destroying guns, gunpowder, and basic necessities that were valued at about $3,000.[67]

As already mentioned, the encroachment on their land plus the killing of seven of their men only reinforced the resentment of the Montserrado leaders toward the American immigrants. But unable to recognize the seriousness of this development, the Americans incautiously and happily went on with the building of their colony. On April 28, 1822, they completed their move to Cape Montserrado where they held a ceremonial celebration for reaching their destiny. Hence, the construction of the town that became Monrovia was begun.[68]

But this increasingly active presence only added to the desire of the Africans to expel the Americans. Dr. Ayres sensed this development and the danger to the colonists. It was against these circumstances and the demoralizing effects of the tropical fever on the immigrants that Dr. Ayres suggested that the immigrants should return to Sierra Leone. One of the surviving black immigrants, Elijah Johnson, rallied the immigrants against Dr. Ayres' suggestion when he made this emotional appeal: "Two years long have I sought a home; here I found one; here I remain."[69]

Johnson's invocation was fortified by the arrival at Monrovia on August 8, 1822, of thirty-six fresh immigrants from America. This group was headed by one Jehudi Ashmun, a deeply religious man from Champlain, New York, who had studied theology and the classics at Middlebury College and the University of Vermont.[70] As will be examined in Chapter IV, he turned out to be one of Liberia's greatest builders.

At this juncture, the immigrants seem to have regained their resolve; and they consequently decided to remain at Cape Montserrado. This did not mean that their problems with the Africans were over. In fact, opposition to their increasing presence was reactivated. Ashmun was among the few white leaders who anticipated that, because of this development, a major confrontation with the Africans was inevitable. He might have arrived at this conclusion partly as a result of his suspicion of the way in which Montserrado was purchased.[71]

With this line of thinking, Ashmun now decided to organize the defense of the settlement. The first task was the clearing of the surrounding bushes. This was mainly carried out to discourage the Africans from secretly penetrating the settlers' defense. As this was being done, an overviewing tower was also constructed to facilitate the location of any military advance by the Africans. In addition to these developments, a group of settlers and some Africans who were friends of the settlers, were being trained as "professional" soldiers to take the main responsibility of defending the settlement. By November of 1822, the settlement was said to be relatively well fortified.[72]

But this development did not actually prohibit the Africans from their military design. Indeed, late in 1822, about eight important chiefs who dwelled around Montserrado created a military alliance with King Peter. The alliance was aimed at expelling the American settlers. This coalition constituted about eight hundred fighting men. They were armed with both African and European weapons.[73]

Well aware that the military strength of the Africans far outweighed that of the American settlers, Ashmun decided to try to deter the former group by telling them:

> He was perfectly apprised with their hostile deliberations, notwithstanding their plans to conceal them; and that, if they proceeded to bring war upon the Americans without even asking to settle differences in a friendly manner, they would dearly learn what it was to fight white men.[74]

This intimidation, however, did not discourage the Africans. Ashmun recognized this, and he, therefore, decided to keep his men on alert for about three days. This precaution was taken in part as a result of information Ashmun had earlier received from his African spies. They had information that an attack on the settlers was imminent. The information was correct, for the attack came on November 11, 1822. The invading African forces succeeded in capturing the western end of the settlement and forced the settlers to retreat to their last stronghold, the immediate area around the overviewing tower. But at this critical juncture, the Africans made a serious tactical mistake: instead of keeping up their military pressure, they now began to loot. Clearly aware of their vulnerablility, the American settlers under the command of Ashmun and his black lieutenant, Reverend Lott Carey, decided to make use of their firepower in full.[75]

The net effect of the settlers' attack on the Africans was fatal. Ashmun described the whole event in this way:

> Imagination can scarcely figure to itself a throng of human beings in more capital state of exposure to destructive power of the machinery of modern warfare! Eight hundred men were here pressed shoulder to shoulder, in so compact a form that a child might easily walk upon their heads from one end of the mass to the other, presenting in their real breadth of rank equal to thirty men, and all exposed to guns of great power raised on a platform, at only thirty to sixty yards distance! Every shot literally spent its force on a solid mass of living human flesh! Their fire suddenly terminated.

> A savage yell was raised which filled the dismal forest with momentary horror. It gradually died away; and the whole host disappeared.[76]

Although the exact number of Africans who died from the above engagement will probably never be known, it was acknowledged that their casualties far outran those of the American settlers. The settlers lost only four persons, and seven of their children were said to have been abducted by the Africans.[77]

Despite this grave setback, the Africans continued to complain that their land had been forcibly taken by the settlers. With no dialogue to address the charge, King Peter and his people decided to attack the settlers for the second time. This was carried out on December 1, 1823. But Ashmun had anticipated this and, accordingly, his men were prepared when the attack came. In fact, the defense of the settlers was better organized at this time than in the preceding clash. With this, and probably because of the demoralizing effect of the first war on the Africans, the settlers were able to defeat them in less than two hours.[78]

This victory over the Africans was a turning point in the historical development of Liberia. It brought about the realization of the desire of the ACS to establish a colony on the coast of West Africa for free blacks in America. Further settlement of such people from the United States could now be carried out in Monrovia and its surrounding areas as the ACS was able confidently to organize the immigration of increasing numbers of settlers.[79]

The victory over the Africans had a further effect of insuring the subordination of the neighboring Africans to the American settlers. From the settlers' point of view, this also meant a triumph over "barbarism." Doubtless, this characterization of the victory was a manifestation of one of the main values that was well inherent in the ACS. The fact that among the paramount objectives of the ACS was to "civilize" Africa bears testimony of this argument. It is not, therefore, surprising that the settlers saw the victory as a beginning of a fulfillment of this desire.[80]

But this characterization of the victory created social conditions whereby the conscious and unconscious internalization of the reluctance to appreciate African values was reinforced among the settlers. The various political, economic, and other social institutions that constituted the development of Liberia were thus more reflective of the settlers' former home of bondage than their newly re-inherited home in Africa. In a way, this was not a sound beginning, and the reasons for this will be examined in the succeeding chapters.

NOTES

Chapter III

[1]See these works about this argument: Fyfe, *A History of Sierra Leone*, pp. 14-19; Henry N. Sherwood, "Early Negro Deportation Projects," pp. 484-508; Richard West, *Back to Africa: A History of Sierra Leone and Liberia* (New York, 1970), pp. 13-68; C. E. Carrington, *The British Overseas: Exploits of a Nation of Shopkeepers* (London, 1968), pp. 130 and 225-226; and Theodore Draper, *The Rediscovery of Black Nationalism* (New York, 1970), pp. 3-14.

[2]For the influence of Paul Cuffe on this, see the subsequent works: Staudenraus, *The American Colonization Movement*, p. 10; Henry N. Sherwood, "Paul Cuffe and His Contribution to the American Colonization Society," *Proceedings of the Mississippi Valley Historical Association*, VI (1912), pp. 153-229; Adelaide C. Hill and Martin Kilson, eds., *Apropos of Africa: Afro-American Leaders and Romance of Africa* (New York, 1971), pp. 11-20; and Peter William, *A Discourse, Delivered on the Death of Captain Paul Cuffe, before the New York African Institution in the African Methodist Episcopal Zion Church, October 21, 1817* (New York, 1817), p. 15.

Actually two other Americans had earlier supported the colonization of black Americans in Africa. They included Dr. William Thornton, a successful Quaker physician, and Samuel D. Hopkins, a preacher of the First Congregational Church in Newport, Rhode Island. Cuffe was, however, the person who made their idea more appealing to later colonizationists. For the details of this explanation, see: Draper, *Rediscovery of Black*, pp. 15-16; Fyfe, *The History of*, p. 112; Sherwood, "Early Negro Deportation Projects," p. 506; and Jordan, *White Over Black*, pp. 550-551.

[3]Jordan, *White Over Black*, pp. 542-559; Shick, *Behold the Promised Land*.

[4]From Bushrod Washington to Samuel J. Mills and Ebenezer Burgess, November 5, 1817, *First Annual Report of the ACS* (1818), pp. 11-12.

[5]West, *Back to Africa*, p. 102.

[6]From Washington to Mills and Burgess, November 5, 1817, *First Annual Report of the ACS*, p. 11.

[7]*Ibid.*, p. 12.

[8]Ralph Gurley, *Life of Jehudi Ashmun* (Washington, 1835), p. 113; from Mills and Burgess (from London) to the ACS, December 30, 1817, *First Annual Report of the ACS*, pp. 70-71.

[9]Hollis Lynch, "Sierra Leone and Liberia in the Nineteenth Century," in J. Ade Ajayi and Ian Espie, eds., *A Thousand Years of*, pp. 331-333.

[10]Alexander, *A History of Colonization*, pp. 100-101.

[11]"Abstract of a Journal of the late Rev. Samuel John Mills," *Second Annual Report of the ACS* (1819), pp. 5-7.

[12]Alexander, *A History of Colonization*, p. 101.

[13]For this argument, see the following works: J. E. Flint, "Chartered Companies and the Scramble for Africa," in Joseph C. Anene and Godfrey N. Brown, eds., *Africa in the Nineteenth and Twentieth Centuries* (Ibadan, 1966), pp. 111-132; Shick, *Behold the Promised Land*, pp. 102-110.

[14]From Mills and Burgess (from London) to the Secretary of the ACS, January 16, 1818, Second Annual Report of the ACS, pp. 69-70.

[15]"Abstract of a Journal" March 26, 1818, *Ibid.*, p. 24.

[16]Alexander, *A History of Colonization*, pp. 102-104.

[17]*Ibid.*, pp. 102-103.

[18]Wadstrom, *Observation on the Slave Trade*, pp. 220-221. There seems to be a disagreement with this explanation. It has been suggested that all the men who were with Ferguson were killed. If this was the case, then Kizell would have been among those killed. See Samuel E. Morison, Henry S. Commager and William Leuchtenburg, *Concise History of the American Republic* (New York, 1983), p. 92 for this argument.

[19]Alexander, *A History of Colonization*, pp. 102-103.

[20]*Ibid.*, p. 103.

[21]"Abstract of a Journal," April 1, 1818, *Second Annual Report of the ACS*, p. 28.

[22]"Abstract of a Journal," April 6, 1818, *Second Annual Report of the ACS*, p. 38; Alexander, *A History of Colonization*, p. 109.

[23]Alexander, p. 109. For similar sayings by later Pan- Africanists, see the following works: C. Legum, *Pan-Africanism: A Short Political Guide* (London, 1962); N. Azikiwe, *The Future of Pan-Africanism* (Lagos, 1964); G. Padmore, *Pan Africanism or Communism*? (Dobson, 1956); M. Garvey, *Philosophy and Opinions*, 2 Vols. (New York, 1926); K. Nkrumah, *Africa Must Unite* (Accra, 1963); W. E. B. Dubois, *Souls of Black Folks* (Chicago, 1903); and Hollis Lynch, *Edward Wilmot Blyden: Pan-Negro Patriot* (London, 1967).

[24]See note 3. This explanation was a response to radical American abolitionists such as W. Garrison, W. Jay, and others who claimed that the ACS' desire was to deport forcibly the free blacks to an unfamiliar land. For details of this argument, see Garrison's *Thoughts on*; Stebbins' *Facts and Opinions*; and Jay's *Inquiry into the Character.*

[25]"Abstract of a Journal," April 23, 1818, *Second Annual Report of the ACS*, p. 56.

[26]*Ibid.*, April 3, 1818, pp. 31-32.

[27]West, *Back to Africa*, pp. 103-104.

[28]"Abstract of a Journal," May 2, 1818, *Second Annual Report of the ACS*, pp. 64-65.

[29]*Ibid.*, April 11, 1818, pp. 43-44.

[30]*Ibid.*, April 3, 1818, p. 32.

[31]*Ibid.*

[32]*Ibid.*, April 4, 1818, p. 35.

[33]*Ibid.*, March 13, 1818, p. 20.

[34]*Ibid.*, March 26, 1818, p. 23.

[35]*Ibid.*, April 4, 1818, pp. 34-35.

[36]*Ibid.*, April 2, 1818, p. 29.

[37]*Ibid.*, April 15, 1818, p. 49.

[38]*Ibid.*, April 2, 1818, pp. 29.

[39]West, *Back to Africa*, pp. 107-109; Shick, *Behold the Promised Land*, pp. 20-24.

[40]Gurley, *Life of Ashmun*, p. 75.

[41]West, *Back to Africa*, p. 108.

[42]Quoted in *Ibid.*

[43]*Ibid.*

[44]Alexander, *A History of Colonization*, p. 120.

[45]*Ibid.*, p. 124.

[46]This has been discussed in detail in Shick's *Behold the Promised Land* and in his "A Quantitative Analysis of Liberian Colonization from 1820 to 1843 with Special Reference to Mortality," *Journal of African History*, VIII (1971), pp. 45-49.

[47]Lieutenant John S. Townsend and Dugan were also white. But their status in relationship to the ACS was not stated. See Alexander, *A History of Colonization*, pp. 121-125.

[48]*Ibid.*, pp. 127-129.

[49]West, *Back to Africa*, p. 107; Shick, *Behold the Promised Land*, pp. 20-22.

[50]*Ibid.*; Alexander, *A History of Colonization*, p. 130.

[51]Shick, *Behold the Promised Land*, p. 23.

[52]Alexander, *A History of Colonization*, pp. 138-140.

[53]*Ibid.*, p. 140.

[54]*Ibid.*, p. 141.

[55]Indeed, most of the early, prominent members of the ACS were not anti-slavery. James Madison, Henry Clay, John Calhoun, and General Harper were, for instance, large slaveholders in America.

[56]Alexander, *A History of Colonization*, p. 141.

[57]*Ibid.*, p. 146-147.

[58]*Ibid.*, p. 147.

[59]See the following works about this concept: Vann Woodward, ed., George Fitzhugh, *Cannibals All*; Jordan, *White over Black*; Genovese, *The World the Slaveholders Made*; Mellon, *Early American Views*; Phillips, *American Negro Slavery*.

[60]Alexander, *A History of Colonization*, p. 156; Shick, *Behold the Promised Land*, p. 23.

[61]West, *Back to Africa*, pp. 112-114; Alexander, *A History of Colonization*, pp. 167-173.

[62]Dr. E. Ayres to ACS, December 11, 1821, *Fifth Annual Report of the ACS* (1822), p. 61.

[63]*Ibid.*, p. 62.

[64]*Ibid.*, pp. 62-63.

[65]West, *Back to Africa*, p. 114.

[66]*Ibid.*, p. 115. "Agreement for the Cession and Purchase of Lands. . . ," *Fifth Annual Report of the ACS*, pp. 64-65. In addition, Anthony J. Nimley has argued that the transaction was illegal. He maintained in a 1977 book that the language used in the transaction, English, was not well understood by King Peter and the other leaders. He argued also that the area which was said to have been bought was not clearly defined. Nimley charged that the original deed which Ayres and Stockton claimed entitled the ACS to Montserrado has not been found. For the details see: Anthony J. Nimley, *The Liberian Bureaucracy: An Analysis and Evaluation of the Environment, Structure, and Functions* (Washington, 1977), pp. 127-137. Similar charges had been made many years earlier in W. Jay's, *Inquiry into the Character and Tendency.*

[67]West, *Back to Africa*, pp. 115-116. See also the following works: S. Wilkeson, *A Concise History of the Commencement, Progress, and Present Condition of the American Colonies in Liberia* (Washington, 1839); E. J. Yancy, *Historical Light of Liberia* (Xenia, 1934); James Young, *Liberia Rediscovered* (New York, 1934).

[68]West, *Back to Africa*, p. 116-119.

[69]*Ibid.*, pp. 116.

[71]*Ibid.*

[72]See the following works: R. Gurley, *Letter to . . . On the Colonization and Civilization of Africa* (London, 1841); R. C. F. Maugham, *The Republic of Liberia* (London, 1929); and West, *Back to Africa*, pp. 118-119.

[73]West, *Back to Africa*, p. 120.

[74]Quoted in *Ibid.*, p. 121.

[75]*Ibid.*; see also Yancy's *Historical Light* and his *Republic of Liberia* (London, 1959).

[76]Quoted in West, *Back to Africa*, p. 122.

[77]*Ibid.*, p. 122.

[78]*Ibid.*

[79]For a detailed treatment of the spread of the settlement on the coast of what became Liberia, see Shick, *Behold the Promised Land*, especially chapters Three, Four, Five, and Six.

[80]As discussed in Chapter I, among the main reasons given by the ACS for its African colonization initiative was the desire to "civilize" Africa. Of course, this meant the extension to Africa of American institutional values, especially Southern institutional values. Such values included Christianity, Old South synthesized social, political, economic and religious culture of paternalism, and other crucial institutional values that deeply influenced the eminent members of the ACS. The above aspect of the ACS has been treated in detail in the following works: Fox, The *American Colonization*; Opper, "The Minds of White Participants;" Sigler, The Attitude of Free Blacks Toward Emigration;" Wickstron, "The American Colonization Society and Liberia;" Forster, "The Colonization of Free Negroes;" Staudenraus, *The African Colonization Movement*; Hodkins, *An Inquiry into the Merits*; Alexander, *A History of Colonization*; Garrison, *Thoughts on the African Colonization*; Stebbins, *Facts and Opinions*; and Gurley, *Mission to England.*

LIBERIA

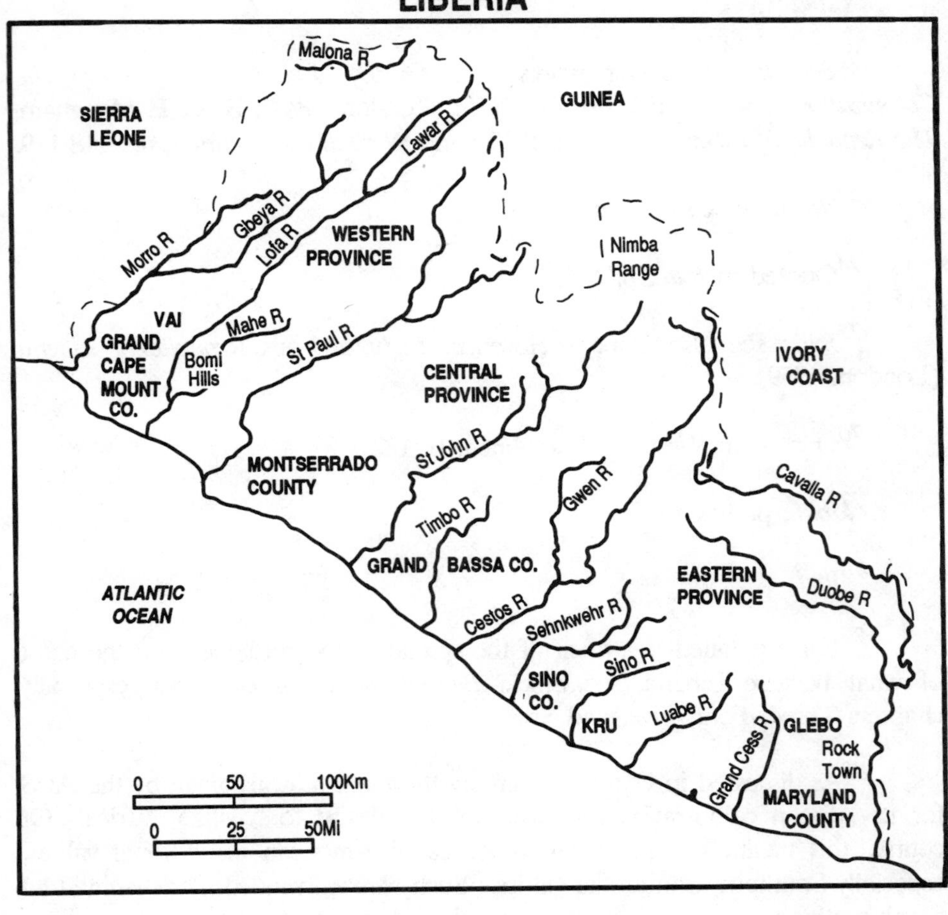
Malona R
SIERRA LEONE
GUINEA
Lawar R
Gbeya R
Morro R
Lofa R
WESTERN PROVINCE
Nimba Range
VAI
Mahe R
GRAND CAPE MOUNT CO.
Bomi Hills
St Paul R
IVORY COAST
CENTRAL PROVINCE
St John R
MONTSERRADO COUNTY
Gwen R
Cavalla R
Timbo R
GRAND
BASSA CO.
EASTERN PROVINCE
Duobe R
ATLANTIC OCEAN
Cestos R
Sehnkwehr R
Sino R
SINO CO.
KRU
Luabe R
GLEBO
Rock Town
Grand Cess R
MARYLAND COUNTY
0
50
100Km
0
25
50Mi

CHAPTER IV

LIBERIAN POLITICAL INSTITUTIONS IMPOSED BY THE AMERICAN COLONIZATION SOCIETY

The institutional developments of Liberia can best be understood by examining them in relation to the African reality and the ACS. Although factors unique to West Africa would play an important role in the evolution of Liberia's political, economic, and social developments, the ACS, after 1822, became the main formulator and determinant. This was particularly demonstrated by the way in which paternalism and power centralization came to be characteristics of the political culture of Liberia. International conditions, especially political and economic relations with Britain and France, played an important part in shaping that political culture as well.

Among the paramount desires of the founders of the ACS was the wish to convey to Liberia institutional values and norms which they esteemed. These included their political, economic, and other social values. It must be pointed out, however, that the passing processes were occasionally executed unconsciously. This could be explained in part by the fact that the social values of the founders of the ACS, like those of most other people, were an integral part of their "social persons."[1] Whether as a result of conscious or unconscious processes, the political organization established by the ACS in Liberia constituted the social characteristics of its prominent founders and administrators.

This was demonstrated by the first representatives the ACS sent to West Africa to begin the settlement process. They became the official conveyors of the ACS' policies and values to that region. When Bacon and two other white representatives accompanied by eighty-eight free blacks sailed from New York to West Africa on January 31, 1820, they thus became the first in a long line of ACS' representatives charged with successfully controlling and shaping the settlers in ways acceptable to the parent body.

Bacon, who was the chief administrator of the sailing immigrants, faced his first major leadership challenge just a week into the voyage. This was brought about by an event which occurred between one of the black immigrants and the captain of the ship. Two dogs, one owned by the former, and the other by the latter, got into a fight. Presumably the dog owned by the black was being beaten by the captain's dog. This development precipitated an angry response from the blacks, which forced the captain to "call for his pistols." A fight between the two parties seemed imminent. But Bacon and his black assistant, Coker, averted a potentially violent situation.[2] While the method employed to pacify the captain was not clearly spelled out in surviving accounts, the one used to appease the blacks was self evident. Bacon showed this when he declared, "Brother Coker, this is an awful judgment come upon us; come let us go below and have religious worship."[3] Obviously, Bacon and his assistant conducted the worship in such a way as to bring the blacks under control. The use of religious appeals to influence blacks did not, however, begin on the ship; the practice was well employed in the slaveholding states, passed on to the ACS, and then to the people who were being sent to West Africa by that movement.[4]

Another administrative legacy was already in the making. Whites would clearly be in control. Coker was one of the most competent members of the first group of immigrants sent by the ACS. Bacon later recognized this when he told Coker "how lucky the expedition was to have him . . . as a middle link between the whites and the coloured people. . . ." Coker replied in kind when he told Bacon that he needed only a "a sable skin to make him an African."[5] Despite the admiration both men had for each other, Coker was never officially appointed "to some position of honour and trust in the new Liberian settlement" prior to the death of Bacon. In fact, the chief administrative responsibilities were passed on to Dr. Ayres and two other whites who arrived from the United States three months after the death of Bacon. This legacy was to continue in Liberia up to the 1840s.[6]

The administration of Dr. Ayres did not last long. Several factors led to this. As noted earlier, the net effect of fever on him and the people he led was the primary reason. Dr. Ayres' incompetent leadership was another factor. In fact, this created conditions which led to a climate of disrespect. It was due to these developments that Dr. Ayres appealed to the settlers to return to Sierra Leone. Although he left the settlement in 1822, Dr. Ayres' call did not succeed in influencing the settlers to follow suit. As discussed earlier, the latter decided to remain. Of course, this was influenced by Elijah Johnson and later reinforced by new immigrants from America. The new arrivals were headed by Jehudi Ashmun, who became a great administrator in the colony.

The administrative policy of the settlement was clearly spelled out when Ashmun assumed leadership in 1822. In his attempt to prepare the settlers for self-defense, Ashmun decided to put them "under military law." He assigned several competent blacks to the following subordinate posts: Johnson became the leader of the colonial stores; R. Sampson was appointed as "Commissery of Ordinance"; and Carey, one of the heroes of the first major war, became the health officer of the settlement. Other blacks were charged with military responsibilities.[7]

Indeed, by virtue of his administrative talent and his successful manipulation of the military threats posed by the Africans, Ashmun succeeded in making himself the sole arbiter of the new power arrangements. His excellent leadership which brought victory to the settlers in 1822 enhanced that development. Despite these achievements, the ACS had not yet officially approved his leadership.[8] The failure to do so was largely the result of the fact that the ACS was not aware of Ashmun's achievements. Dr. Ayres, who had left the settlement in 1822 but was still recognized as the legitimate chief administrator of the settlement, contributed to this. He had written a letter to the ACS early in 1823, distorting Ashmun's achievements and minimizing his own failures.[9]

Dr. Ayres' main desire was to undermine Ashmun, which he in fact succeeded in doing. After the ACS received his letter, the American body empowered Dr. Ayres to return from Sierra Leone and deprive Ashmun "of all authority in the settlement."[10] With Ayres' return, Ashmun lost his authority, and he decided to turn to trade. He gave as his reason for this: ". . . I have debts to pay and money must be raised."[11]

Developments soon brought Ashmun back to power. Dr. Ayres, who now resumed leadership of the settlement, was not doing better than before. He for example, forcibly implemented the disliked new plan of Monrovia which had been blue-printed in Washington, D.C.[12] While Dr. Ayres saw this as an execution of an order sent to him by the ACS, the settlers viewed it as an infringement on their rights. They had a reason to perceive it in that manner. The implementation of the new town plan meant a relocation of the settlers who were already established. Besides, the first group of settlers opposed Dr. Ayres' policy of distributing food and other supplies evenly among the settlers. This opposition was directed against the new arrivals who the former group accused of not having suffered enough to receive the full benefit of the settlement. Declining health, coupled with the outlined problems, forced Dr. Ayres to leave the settlement in early 1823, and he never returned.[13]

Ashmun once more assumed authority following Ayres' departure; but the administrative problems he inherited continued. The practice of food rationing introduced by Dr. Ayres was not revoked by Ashmun. Besides, his desire to impress the ACS led him to reinforce the disliked policy of land allotment. Ashmun added insult to injury when he demanded that all adult male settlers must provide two days of "public work" and he warned that those who did not do so would not receive food and other supplies provided by the ACS.[14] Indeed, resentment toward Ashmun was intensified when, on March 19, 1823, he reduced the ration to half.[15] These actions, together with no attempt at compromise, led the settlers to attack and loot the colonial stores. They also wrote a letter to the ACS charging Ashmun with corruption, favoritism, and nepotism.[16]

With no physical means at his disposal to discipline the settlers, Ashmun decided to appeal paternalistically to them in these words:

> There is a mutual contract subsisting between the American colonization society and every one of you. . . . You swore to the Society that you would obey your

> government and not attempt to overthrow it. . . . Every blessing you have enjoyed in Africa, the security of your lives, property and families, is the consequence of this statutory arrangement by which anefficient government was constituted. . . . Some of your sufferings have resulted from your disrespect to the Agent. . . . But you have nothing in possession. You have nothing growing in your fields. You have nothing--not a week's supply of vegetables in prospect. . . . Continue to neglect your duty, and it will either disperse you up and down the coast or destroy you by starvation. . . . I ask you to take no new oaths, to assume no new obligations; but here this hours, in the presence of that God who has recorded your vows in Heaven to recognize them and pledge yourselves to a future observance of them.[17]

Ashmun had hoped to bring tranquility to the settlement through his appeal, but he did not. Some of the reasons for this have already been given. Ashmun's failure to repudiate the administrative policies of his predecessor was one of the main reasons for his problems. But this was only one of several reasons; following the final departure of Dr. Ayres, the ACS decided not to supply the settlers with basic necessities. This, and the fact that the settlers were taking a united stand, showed that Ashmun did not have the material and physical means to influence developments in the settlement. No wonder the appeal did not succeed in accomplishing its objective. In fact, Carey, who had been Ashmun's main assistant during the last two wars, joined the opposition that threatened the authority of the latter in late 1823.[18]

Despite this mounting opposition, Ashmun refused to give in easily. Early in 1824, for example, he wrote the ACS charging the settlers with insubordination. In response, the ACS wrote to Ashmun requesting that he employ drastic measures in administering the settlement. He was to "punish any insolence with summary fines or imprisonment." The reply also stipulated that "if need arose," he "should call in support from a ship of the United States Navy."[19] But before these mandates reached Ashmun, he had already been forced out of the settlement by the settlers. Ashmun escaped to the Cape

Verde Islands where he was received by Ralph R. Gurley, who had been sent by the ACS to investigate developments in the settlement.[20]

This was not, however, the end of Ashmun's administration. In fact, he returned to the settlement in April 1824, and he reassumed the same administrative position he held before his departure. By this time, the hostile attitude of the settlers was giving way to a conciliatory one. This development created an atmosphere which made the administering of the settlement easier. This improvement had been enhanced by Gurley, the special envoy of the ACS. From the Cape Verde Islands, both men sailed to the Liberian settlement. During their voyage, Ashmun succeeded in dismissing all the doubts about his administrative ability. He thoroughly convinced Gurley to reappoint him as the chief administrator of the settlement, despite the fact that the ACS had warned its envoy not to carry out such a design.[21] Ashmun was also advised to be more flexible and conciliatory toward the settlers.

As he worked to reconsolidate Ashmun's authority, Gurley tactfully created a condition to make his design more acceptable to the settlers. He played down, for example, the ACS' recommendation to prosecute all the ringleaders of the opposition that occurred in the settlement. To create a sense among the settlers that they were part of the government that led them, Gurley, together with Ashmun, set up a council composed of members of the settlers to assist in the running of the government.[22] Despite the establishment of the council, the power of the chief administrator in the colony, now represented by Ashmun continued to be predominant.

Although these initiatives were not approved by the ACS, their net result, when combined with the economic leverage Gurley was able to provide, brought tranquility and prosperity to the settlement. The settlers again began to treat Ashmun with respect.[23] With this, the defense of the settlement was refortified under the supervision of Ashmun. Besides, farm lands were enlarged, thus creating a sense of self-reliance among the settlers. Moreover, Ashmun and Gurley were able to provide more material rewards. Gurley was able to ensure supplies of food, clothing, and building materials, and Ashmun was then able to use the distribution of these goods to build support for his position as leader.[24] The selective use of such material rewards was an important factor in the reestablishment of Ashmun's authority, and the process would indeed become part of Liberian political life.

With this progress, the ACS decided to reward both Ashmun and Gurley. It appointed Ashmun as a "permanent" chief administrator of the settlement and Gurley as a secretary of the ACS. In addition to this responsibility, the United States government authorized Ashmun to administer all the recaptives sent to the settlement by its officers.[25] This provided him with additional funds for the development and defense of the settlement and for buttressing his own political position.

With the settlement well protected, Ashmun decided to direct his attention elsewhere. A new camp for the recaptives and four additional colonial warehouses were erected.[26] Indeed, an elegant mansion, valued at about $7,500 worth of construction materials including yellow pine from the United States, was built for Ashmun.[27] In fact, between 1825 and 1828, the population of settlers increased from 66 to 633 persons. The decline in the death rate brought about by improvements in health, agriculture, and shelter, together with the stability of the settlement, enabled the new arivals to survive better.[28] Of course, these developments were largely brought about by the new leadership introduced by Gurley and promoted by Ashmun in the settlement.

As the population of the settlement expanded, the ACS framed a new constitution for the Liberian colony. The constitution formally established the position of chief administrator of the settlement. This position was to be occupied by an appointee of the ACS, and was to be subject only to that body. Although it allowed the settlers to nominate individuals annually for subordinate positions, the constitution maintained that the decision concerning who could finally occupy such positions was to be determined by the chief administrator. The posts in question included the vice-governor, or second-in-command to the chief administrator, the council or the legislative-like body of the government, the committee of agriculture, public works, militia, and health. The "standing army" that was composed of fifteen men, the judiciary, and other positions of importance, "remained under the direct control" of the chief administrator, later called governor. With the help of the council, whose members included the vice governor and two other persons who were indirectly elected to the council, the governor had the constitutional authority to deal with issues that were uncovered "by common law or the constitution . . . ." Issues of paramount importance such as foreign affairs and the "sovereignty" of the settlement, however, rested with the ACS.[29]

The constitution also covered other issues of significance. It served as a social determinant and a castigator to those settlers who failed to conform to the social values set for them by the ACS. Those who rioted or were caught drunk or did not strictly observe the Sabbath, for example, were stockaded and occasionally whipped. No one could reside in the colony without the authorization of the governor. A settler family could not "own more than ten acres," nor could a non-permanent resident own land in the colony. Missionaries could stay in the colony if they limited themselves to non-secular issues.[30] One could not trade in the colony without the endorsement of the governor. An amendment to the constitution was made in 1825.[31] Instead of candidates being nominated for offices, they would now be elected by manhood suffrage though the governor still had the final say.[32]

This constitutional arrangement clearly showed that the vast power of the governor did not derive from the settlers; rather, it came from the ACS which was some 5,000 miles away. Hence, the fact that the governor had the consitutional authorization to determine nearly all political initiatives, to reward social conformists, clearly illustrated that he was supremely powerful. No wonder he was so feared by some and resented by others, as this description bears testimony:

> Mr. Ashmun stood among the colonists like a father in the midst of his children. Affection tempered his authority and respect dignified their obedience. His wisdom and firmness won their confidence, while his confidence in them increased as he beheld them inclined to instruction and deriving profit from experience. The bond which so united him to this little community was strengthened by recollection of mutual cares, interests, labours, sufferings, sympathies, and dangers.[33]

This description had, however, an opposite side. As noted, the settlers expelled Ashmun from the settlement and Gurley later reinstated him. One may wonder why the very settlers who opposed him at one time admired him at another. This question has already been answered in part. As in the Old South, paternalism in Liberia was designed to reward those who conformed to the established social values and norms, or who accepted the patriarchal type of authority, and to chastise those who did not. This was clearly demonstrated when the settlers forced Ashmun out of the settlement. As noted, after his expulsion Ashmun wrote the ACS indicting the settlers for insubordination. The ACS reacted swiftly and drastically. It withheld food and other basic necessities designated for the settlement.[34] The aim of this action was clear, and the result was as the ACS had expected. The settlers came to see that their hostility to Ashmun was responsible for the refusal of the ACS to send them supplies. Acceptance of Ashmun's authority led to the resumption of crucial supplies. His selective use of them enhanced his position of leadership even further as it allowed him to reward those loyal to him and to punish those opposed to his policies. These factors, together with the more relaxed policy introduced by Gurley, influenced the setters to give in to Ashmun.[35]

It is, therefore, not suprising that the ACS continued to propagate such a system of administration and its associated values inherent in paternalism. They were effective in controlling blacks in the Old South and in the settlement, even though in both places they were violently opposed.[36] The appointment of a non-black for the governorship throughout most of the early history of Liberia[37] corresponded, moreover, with the widely held paternalistic concept that blacks were children and as such needed the protection of someone from the "master class."[38]

In addition, the ACS took steps, as time passed, to further strengthen the power of the executive. During the administration of Thomas Buchanan, who served as the last white Governor of Liberia (1839-1841), an amendment to the constitution was made. This was designed to empower the governor to arrest the insubordination of some Africans and a group of settlers who had established some small outposts around Monrovia. But the strengthening of the governor's authority only reinforced the dictatorial political structure the ACS had already commenced in the settlement. Despite this, Governor Buchanan felt that he did not have enough power to execute the various administrative policies. In 1840, for instance, he wrote to the ACS deploring that "the great error in our system of government is the infusion of the principle of democracy."[39] But as he made these complaints, he was weakened and finally killed by fever in 1841.

Buchanan was succeeded as governor by one of the settlers, Joseph J. Roberts;[40] this development, however, did not mean that the political legacy introduced in Liberia by the ACS came to an end. Quite the contrary, it continued to be an integral part of the historical development of that country up to the present century. Although he was considered black, Roberts' administrative policies were the same as those of his white predecessors. This should not be surprising, as some earlier and contemporary scholars on Liberia would have people to believe.[41] Before he became governor in 1841, Roberts was already a member of the upper stratum of the emerging social stratifications in Liberia. He was born in Norfolk, Virginia, in 1809. He was a very light-skinned black. Later, he and his mother decided to move to Petersburg, Virginia, where they joined the "free Afro-American community."[42] In Petersburg, Roberts and one William N. Colson, a free black with some property holdings, founded a business venture. It brought commercial and later political success to Roberts in Liberia.[43] Upon his arrival in Liberia in 1829, Roberts, like Carey, Ashmun and others who had brought some capital from America with them, immediately began to involve himself with trade. This brought him tremendous wealth. As a member of an evolving privileged class, Roberts was appointed a sheriff and later trained as a militia officer, a position that allowed him to demonstrate his leadership ability by his victory over the Gola African ethnic group. His victory saved the Deys, an African ethnic group who were allies of the American settlers, from defeat.[44]

Besides his ingenuity and industriousness, it could be equitably argued that Roberts' success was also enhanced by his parental background which was basically influenced by the legacy of the Old South. That legacy gave preferential consideration to the mulattoes who served as a "buffer" between masters and slaves. Hence, the masters' consanguineous relationship with the mulattoes impelled them to be morally and socially more considerate to the latter than of the dark-skinned blacks who largely made up the slave population. This was influenced in part by the thought that anything closer to the values of the master class, both in appearance and spirit, was more appropriate than the one that was not.[45] In return, the mulattoes, like most social groups in a similar situation, tended to identify themselves with the values of the master class more than those of the oppressed class, since the former, if properly exploited, would guarantee achievement.[46] In their identifying process, the mulattoes were not allowed, however, to fulfill their own initiatives or innovations, for it was feared that this would jeopardize the legacy. This rigidly applied to those initiatives the master class conceived as potentially dangerous to the status quo.[47] This was why Governor Roberts and all who succeeded him continued to be mostly consumers or implementers of the institutional values commenced by the ACS in Liberia. They were not formulators of those values as some distorted interpretations of Liberian history maintain.[48] This together with Roberts' business success and, above all, his strong devotion to and articulation of the values introduced by the ACS in Liberia thus led to his appointment as governor in 1841. No wonder the ACS officially endorsed his appointment in the following year.[49]

When Roberts became governor, Liberia's political formation was taking on a more complex form. Although political parties in the American sense did not exist, Liberia did have political factions whose members articulated specific political views. This development was reinforced by several factors. As discussed, Ashmun had been accused of favoring certain settlers. This charge was not lacking evidence. Ashmun had favored the mulattoes and the few educated dark-skinned blacks. This was clearly shown by his unfair assignments of lands and political positions.[50] Ashmun, personally, was not the originator of this system; it had been inherent in the background of the ACS, carried to the coast of pre-Liberia, and advanced by the various chief administrators of colonial Liberia. By the end of Governor Buchanan's administration, the practice of favoring the mulattoes had reached the point where it was increasingly dividing the settlement into two main opposing camps.

The injustice of this system was indirectly exposed by one Reverend John Seys of the Methodist Episcopal Church. During Buchanan's governorship, he had asked whether it was fair for his

Church to pay duties on goods it imported.[51] Although it was recommended to the Supreme Court of the settlement, the charge turned out to be more than just a "legal" issue. Following this, dark-skinned black petty farmers from small settlements such as Millsburg, Bassa Cove, and Edina began to side with Seys, though for political reasons.[52]

This was clearly manifested during the election of new members to the Colonial Council in 1840. During that election, settlers from these settlements wanted to elect people to the Council who they assumed would continually identify with their interests. Although an amendment to the constitution in 1839 allowed for this, it did not undermine the other alternatives the governor had to make his influence felt on the Council. While it stipulated that the settlers could elect three persons to the Council, the amendment also maintained that the three elected officials and the governor were allowed to elect five additional people to the Council. Monrovia, permanent residence of the governor, provided three members.[53]

This constitutional arrangement actually reinforced the political supremacy of the governor, since most politicians in Monrovia tended to side with him. More important, the governor continued to control substantial resources with which to reward those who supported him. His predominant role was further ensured by the fact that he was empowered to preside over all meetings of the Council and to veto any proposal introduced by that body. Besides, he had constitutional authorization to cast the deciding vote on issues on which the Council was equally divided. It must be added that the governor's tremendous power came directly from the ACS, and only that organization could remove him from his position.[54]

Frustrations with these arrangements caused settlers from Millsburg, Bassa Cove, and Edina to protest against Buchanan's policies and to support candidates for the Colonial Council who identified with their causes. Even religious groups, especially those from Seys' church, emphasized a political tone, and several public gatherings were held during which resolutions directed against Governor Buchanan and his administration were introduced and passed. Seys was quoted as saying that "citizens ought to rise up and shuck off this rotten system of tyranny and oppression."[55] Despite these attacks, the political factions that supported Governor Buchanan managed to win a majority of the seats in the Council in the 1840 elections. This was probably influenced by the fact that the administration had at its disposal many means, including money, political positions, intimidation and, above all, the enormous power of the governor to determine the outcome of the election.[56]

The defeat of Seys' forces did not mean that political opposition faded. In fact, just before he became governor in 1841, Roberts and others who supported Buchanan in the Colonial Council introduced and passed bills which barred Seys and his groups from criticizing the government.[57] This demonstrated both the power of the colonial administration and the fact that there was increasing opposition to it. It must, however, be pointed out that there was also a need for political unity, and Roberts quickly took advantage of this to consolidate his new positon as governor.

The need for political unity became quickly apparent since the beginning of Governor Roberts' administration coincided with increased commercial activities by the British and French on the coast of Liberia. Because of this, Governor Roberts decided to establish control over the coastal area between Cape Mount and the settlement of Maryland which still existed as an independent entity from the Liberian settlement.[58] Through a treaty with King Yoda of the Gola in 1843 and a similar one with other local chiefs in 1845, Governor Roberts succeeded in gaining possession of the coastal area that extended from the Mano River in the northwest to the Grand Cester River in the southeast. About the same time, Maryland, which was located on the southeast of Liberia, expanded its coastal area some sixty miles east of Cape Palmas, its chief town (see map p. 104).[59] As suggested, the main objective of these undertakings was to arrest the increasing advance of the British and French traders on the coasts of the two settlements. Prior to this expansion, the two colonies maintained that "foreign vessels" could trade only at certain "ports of entry," and they would have to pay "an ad valorem duty of six percent" in order to do so.[60]

While this policy made heroes of both Governors Roberts and John B. Russwurm of Maryland and eased the development of political tensions in their respective settlements, it precipitated an immediate response from the British and French. Their reaction was initially directed against Liberia, because its coastal policy affected a larger area than Maryland's. The British soon protested through the Governor of Sierra Leone Liberia's coastal policy:

> The right . . . of imposing custom duties could only be lawfully exercised by sovereign and independent states. . . . I need not remind your Excellency that this description does not yet apply to Liberia which is not yet recognized as a subsisting state even by the Government of the country from which its settlers have immigrated. . . .[61]

With this, British traders stationed in Sierra Leone declared that they would not pay any tax to the two colonies nor would they honor their united port of entry policy.[62]

Governor Roberts, on the other hand, decided to reinforce his position. In 1845, he ordered the seizure of a British vessel for refusing to pay the port of entry fees. The British in Sierra Leone responded by sending to Monrovia a gunboat which attacked and apprehended a vessel owned by Allen Banson, a prosperous settler trader who later became Liberia's president (1856-1864).

In response, Governor Roberts wrote to the ACS explaining in detail what he termed British infringement on the fundamental rights of Liberia.[63] The ACS finally brought the whole issue to the attention of the United States government.[64] But the United States' lagging and passive attitude toward the issue seems to have influenced the British Foreign Office to respond assertively.[65] In fact, the British informed the United States that it "could not accept the slightest assumption of any sovereign powers being present in a commercial experiment of a Philanthropic society." With no desire to anger the British, the Americans demanded no further explanation from the former,[66] but instead warned the Liberian authorities that the "operations of British traders were backed by the British Navy."[67]

At this juncture, it became clearly known to the Liberian leaders that the "sovereignty" they had assumed was far from a reality. Against this background, the supreme desire of Governor Roberts was to declare the independence of Liberia. This sentiment was to rally nearly all Liberian settlers behind Governor Roberts and his administration from 1844 to 1847.

The yearning for independence was soon reinforced by the ACS. During June of 1846, the ACS informed Governor Roberts that "the time has arrived when it was expedient for the people of the Commonwealth of Liberia to take into their own hands the whole work of self-government, including the management of their foreign relations."[68] With this directive, Governor Roberts told the colonists that Liberia could not possibly survive without declaring its independence. This warning was immediately framed as a proposal and submitted to the Council and "passed and adopted by a majority" of that body on October 7, 1846.[69] The minority who opposed the bill were mostly representatives from the settlements outside the vicinity of Monrovia, the mainstay of power. They rightly reasoned that if independence was won at that time, Monrovia would continue to dominate the emerging power structure.[70] But despite this opposition, the bill won the support of nearly every settler. This was even true of those who had earlier opposed the administration of Governor Roberts.

Some of the reasons for this broad-based support have already been noted. The ACS, the British, and the American governments were directly and indirectly pressuring Liberia to declare its independence. Added to this was the fact that the idea associated with independence was giving rise to settler nationalism. Governor Roberts, who spearheaded Monrovia's establishment, successfully exploited this to promote his call for independence. No wonder the settlers popularly sanctioned the appeal which finally led to the declaration of Liberia's independence in 1847.[71]

On July 26, 1847, a modified[72] historical process was begun in Liberia. On that date, a convention was held, and it was followed by the declaration of independence of Liberia. The thirteen representatives who attended the convention came from the following political subdivisions: Montserrado, Grand Bassa, and Sinoe counties. The numbers of representatives a county could send was determined by the population and the political leverage that the county had. Montserrado, which was the seat of the colonial government and the most populous settlement, for example, sent six representatives. It was followed by Grand Bassa which sent five, and Sinoe, which was a newly created county, sent only one representative. Samuel Benedict, who later became Chief Justice of Liberia, was appointed to preside over the convention, and in addition, one Joseph Prouts from the colony of Maryland which was still separated from Liberia, served as the convention's secretary.[73] It must be added that nearly all the representatives came from the property holding class.[74] This was to influence the political development of Liberia.

At the convention, the reasons for the declaration of independence were clearly spelled out. The declaration read in part:

> We the representatives of the people of the commonwealth of Liberia in convention assembled, invested with the authority of forming a new government, relying upon the aid and protection of the Great Arbiter of human events, do hereby in the name and behalf of the people of this commonwealth, publish and declare the said commonwealth a free, sovereign, and independent state by the name and title of the Republic of Liberia. . . . We recognize in all men certain inalienable rights; among these are life, liberty, and right to acquire, possess, enjoy, and secure their rights. . . . We the people of the Republic of Liberia were originally inhabitants of the United States of North America. In some parts of that country we were debarred by laws from all rights and privileges of man--in other parts public sentiment more powerful than law frowned down on us. We were excluded from all participation in the government. We were taxed without our consent. We were compelled to contribute to the resources of a country which gave us no protection. . . . Strangers from other lands of a color different from ours, were preferred before us. We uttered our complaints, but they were unattended. Liberia is not the offspring of ambition, nor the tool of

avaricious speculation. . . . Liberia is an asylum from the most grinding oppression.[75]

Evidently, this declaration, like the American Declaration of Independence, was an expression of what its framers considered a genuine reason for the establishment and the expression of the independence of Liberia.[76] Indeed, a more elaborate form of the declaration was manifested by the new Liberian constitution that was framed immediately after that country affirmed its independence. The constitution was a replica of that of the United States. It emphasized the basic rights of adult black men, and like the latter, it limited eligibility to high political office and the right to vote to those who had property.[77] In addition, the power structure of the proposed government was divided into legislative, executive, and judicial branches, each with equal power. The framers of the constitution made this arrangement mainly to maintain power equilibrium among the three key branches of the government. This array did not work for long; the executive branch increasingly became predominant.

The constitution was approved by September 1847, and Governor Roberts was elected president of the new country by January 1848. But the forces that had pressed the settlers to unite politically were giving way to a reemerging social expediency. This development actually began immediately after independence was declared. As noted, other settlers resented the continued political and social domination of the Montserrado settlers. The oppositon, however, was nullified by the various increasing demands for Liberia to declare its independence. Now that independence was declared, the tensions that had existed between the adversary groups resurfaced.

Unlike the tensions of pre-independent Liberia, those of independent Liberia were clearly manifested in the forms of party politics. In fact, the newly elected president had been backed by a party called the True Liberian Party (TLP), later to be ordained the Republican Party (RP). The renaming was designed to counteract an opposition political group that became known as the Old Whig Party (OWP). The latter party, which was composed mostly of poor settlers, increasingly gained numerical support over the TLP that constituted primarily well-to-do settlers. This was enhanced by the fact that the

OWP identified itself with the common settlers, who outnumbered the privileged mulattoes and their few dark-skinned black allies, the main constituents of the TLP. To avert the danger of losing power, the TLP decided to rename itself the RP, for it was anticipated that this would be more appealing to the new arrivals from America, who were likely to approve, especially in the early 1860s, the program of the Republican Party in the United States.[78]

Such a strategy was probably unnecessary for the RP to continue in power from 1847 to 1869. The reason for this has already been explained in part. The ACS created social conditions whereby the mulattoes and their handful of educated dark-skinned black counterparts who continually identified with that organization inherited nearly all the crucial institutions just before independence was declared. The members of the two groups included eminent merchant settlers like Roberts, Carey, F. Devancy, C. M. Waring, and R. A. Sherman. These representatives of the propertyowning class had dominated the Colonial Council and passed bills designed to subdue their opponents.[79] The new constitution further fortified this by overwhelmingly concentrating nearly all the significant political institutions in the hands of the elites. Furthermore, elite members from this class who had the potential to defect were either discouraged from this through political rewards, or punished if such inducements failed. Benedict, who had presided over the convention, turned out to be a rival candidate to Governor Roberts during that presidential race. Having defeated his rival, Roberts quickly appointed Benedict Chief Justice of Liberia.[80] It is not surprising, therefore, that the OWP did not gain political supremacy until 1869. As a party of the "commoners," it did not have the material resources that were essentially needed to give political leverage to its numerical strength.

Although it did not capture the presidency until 1869, the OWP continued to remain an opposing force. In fact, every Republican president who served from 1847 to 1869 was forced to reckon with this. Of course, the Republicans' domination and the social values that this domination rationalized and reinforced were behind the opposition, as was later noted by A. Karnga:

> Dissatisfaction and discontent were rife among the people through the misrule of the Republican Party . . . . The official classes now regarded themselves as patricians, while the masses or common people or the Americo-Liberians, including the Congoes, were looked upon as plebians in the Old Roman sense. The original population or natives, were not by then considered at all. Society therefore became divided into four distinct orders: the official class including the big traders, the common people, the Congoes, and the natives. Social intercourse and marriage amongst these groups were by custom forbidden. Men of light complexion were moreover preferred to their brothers in ebony. The Republicans held that the climate was more severe on the colonists with lighter complexions than on the blacks, and for this reason, the pure blacks should go to the soil for subsistence, whilst as their brothers with blue veins should remain in the Government offices to conduct the affairs of state.[81]

Despite such social arrangements and justifications, the Republicans could not have stayed in power as long as they did had they not been successful in manipulating the values introduced by the ACS and the threats posed to the sovereignty of Liberia by Britain and France. In his first inaugural address, for example, President Roberts emphatically played upon the religious sentiment that had been introduced in Liberia by the ACS. He declared that "the redemption of Africa from deep degradation, superstition, and idolatry in which she has been so involved" should be carried forward.[82] In his third inaugural speech, he again emphasized that " . . . it is very evident that the establishment of this Republic was not wholly the work of man. . . . Yes, gentlemen, Heaven had declared it, and the decree has gone forth, not to be recalled: Ethiopia shall stretch forth her hands unto God!"[83] He had earlier appealed to the people to support his government since, according to him, it was among the designs of God.

But President Roberts not only followed the formula of earlier ACS'governors in using the appeal of religion to rally the people behind his government; he used foreign threats as well. In 1851, he charged, for instance, that occasionally European traders "have not reciprocated our friendly disposition, but by unjustifiable conduct have given occasion of just indignation," thus instilling "in certain chiefs the spirit of insubordination."[84]

President Roberts' charge did not lack evidence. In 1851, a British trader from Sierra Leone told a group of indigenous Africans in the southwestern part of Liberia that their land was being stolen by the new Liberian government.[85] In 1860, John M. Harris, another British merchant based in Sierra Leone, was caught trading illegally in an area bought by Liberia in 1848. When the Liberian government accused him of this, he arrogantly dismissed the charge by declaring that "Liberia's customs dues would upset the trade of the interior. . . ."[86] Liberia reacted by seizing two of the vessels Harris employed in the trade.

But these measures precipitated a counterresponse from the British. As before, the British dispatched to Monrovia a gunboat thus forcing the Liberian government to release the two vessels.[87] With no army or navy to match those of the European powers, Liberia had little choice but to give in to the British demands and rely heavily on diplomacy. Indeed, Liberia's presidents who served during the period under study attached great value to diplomacy even though it did not stop the Europeans from transgressing the sovereignty of Liberia.[88]

This external pressure did, however, help to mitigate opposition against the continued domination of the RP. Appeals could be made to Liberian nationalism as a means of keeping such opposition in check.

This did not mean that the OWP was no longer a threat to be reckoned with. The fact that all Republican presidents who served from 1847 to 1869 warned of the threat of disunity and hostility gives evidence of this. Daniel B. Warner (1864-1868), gave a clear example of this in his inaugural speech. He emphasized that:

> I have noticed with emotions of deep regret what I considered indications of a growing feeling of sectionalism among us, manifested particularly within the last few weeks. Need I say that in every point of view, whether

> affecting the social condition, the material property, or the civil liberty of our country, sectionalism is an unmitigated curse. I sincerely trust every such feeling will be at once put down among us, for it cannot but exercise a deep and widespread influence for evil and only evil continually.[89]

In a similar way, James S. Payne (1868-1870), who succeeded President Warner, maintained that the anti-attitude toward the government by certain individuals would influence others which might finally lead to the destruction of the country.[90]

Despite these warnings, opposition to the RP increasingly surfaced. In fact, on January 7, 1869, the OWP, the main opposition, held a convention at a place called Caldwell, and renamed itself the National True Whig Party (NTWP). The convention was said to be one of the largest political gatherings in the history of Liberia.[91] It was led by prominent dark-skinned politicians such as Edward J. Roye, James L. Smith, and Edward Blyden, an intellectual and eminent pan-Africanist. The party appointed Roye as its presidential candidate and Smith as vice presidential candidate for the election that was to be held that year. During the convention, the Whigs emphasized that the position that "I can't or we can't" should be replaced by "I will or we will try." The party seems to have emphasized this to refute the view held by some of its supporters that the Whigs could never capture the presidency. The Republicans were accused of using skin color as a canon for political appointments.[92] The issue of corruption was also brought out. The Whigs charged the Republicans with circumventing the constitution in order to continue in power. To substantiate this allegation, the Whigs argued that the Republicans occasionally set aside money from the national treasury for the sole purpose of winning elections.[93]

In his acceptance speech, vice-presidential candidate Smith spelled out the main aims of the party:

> I understand the . . . broad principles of our constitution and projecting the bold measures for the speedy improvement of the country, and for the speedy development of its resources, the creation of banks, the production of good

> circulating medium whereby the arm of industry and enterprise will be strengthened and the nation will become strong, prosperous, happy, the means and facilities will then be at hand to give law and Gospel, Church, and State to Africa. I could not find it in my heart to decline the honor done me.[94]

With such objectives pleasing to many Liberians, the NTWP succeeded in winning the presidential election of 1869. It could be maintained that this first victory was a manifestation of the general disapproval of the performances of the various Republican administrations from 1847 to 1869. But this did not mean the institutional values introduced in Liberia by the ACS, and inherited and perfected by the Republicans, would be done away with. In his first inaugural speech, President Roye (1870-1871) emphasized the same institutional values his predecessors had earlier stressed. Like them all, Roye saw Liberia as God's creation, and with this, he reemphasized that the foremost task before Liberia was to spread the words of God throughout the country.[95] Even his civil initiatives were influenced by this. He maintained in the same speech:

> I believe that the erection of a railroad will have wonderful influence in the civilization and elevation of the native tribes. The barriers of heathenism and superstition will disappear before the railroad and its concomitants as frost, snow, and ice dissolve before a summer's sun. This is one of the most efficient means by which God's promise made concerning Africa is, in my opinion, to be fulfilled.[96]

Despite the fact that his policies did not differ radically from those of his predecessors, President Roye did not remain in office to finish his term. In 1871, a mob, composed predominantly of mulattoes, attacked the presidential mansion and arrested Roye. The president was later put in prison where he died mysteriously.[97] The enmity that brought this fate to President Roye was a result of several factors. He was the first dark-skinned black to capture the presidency. This radically contradicted the inherited legacy which reinforced the concept that the upper layer of the social stratifications of Liberia was to be continually monopolized by the mulatto social group. It is not, therefore, surprising that Roye's administration was covertly and overtly sabotaged by the light-skinned elites.[98] But it is fair to argue that President Roye contributed to his own downfall. As will be discussed in the next chapter, his attempt to develop Liberia rapidly led that country into great indebtedness to Britain. This and his intention to expand the presidential term from two to four years contributed to his death. The latter was perhaps most serious as it posed a threat to the constitution.[99]

Following the death of Roye in 1871, Vice-President Smith completed his term. In the next presidential election, former President Roberts was reelected on the RP ticket for his fifth term. This victory launched the Republicans on a period of power which lasted until 1877 when the NTWP recaptured the presidency, and from that date, it never lost any presidential election until it was overthrown in a military coup led by Master Sergeant Kanyon Doe on April 12, 1980.[100]

But the reemergence of the NTWP as a powerful force called into being a modified political culture that was to have a lasting impact on the political history of Liberia. Up until the end of the 1870s independent Liberia had a two party political system. But during the administration of President H. R. Johnson (1883-1892), the Whigs succeeded in making Liberia a one-party state. No doubt this development was influenced by several factors. The seizure of almost half of Liberia by Britain and France in the 1880s reinforced the desire of the leaders of that country for political unity. The world economic depression of the same period also indirectly contributed to this need. The fact that the economic collapse disrupted the reliance of the Liberian elites on world commerce forced them to tax heavily the indigenous Africans. This in turn precipitated a series of revolts from the indigenous Africans--revolts that unquestionably reinforced the elites' inclination toward political unity.[101]

It could, therefore, be argued that a one-party system was introduced in Liberia as a response to a compelling need for unity against both internal and external pressures. Of course, this was nothing but a political culture with which Liberia was already familiar. This political centralization, now exemplified by the NTWP, closely resembled, for example, the one the ACS had earlier introduced in the Liberian colony. Like the administration commenced by the ACS, the NTWP had virtual control over all the governmental and nearly all the important non-governmental positions. The latter included "the staff of the College of Liberia . . . heads of churches," and those who were in the newspaper business. These positions were in the patronage of the party, and the chief executive, as standard bearer of the party, served as the main distributor of such positions. This explains why the executive branch of the government became more powerful than both the legislative and judicial branches. This legacy continues in Liberia up to the present.[102]

As has been argued throughout this chapter, however, the politics of patronage as a modified form of paternalism was not begun by the NTWP; it was started by the ACS, inherited by its governors, and promoted by both Republicans and Whigs. The system which was well perfected by the NTWP did manage to abolish the "racial-political" tension that existed between the mulattoes and dark-skinned blacks before the end of the nineteenth century. Having thus united themselves politically, the settler Liberians continued to view the indigenous Liberians as their most threatening internal opponents. But in a way, this was a grave error, for it only buttressed the hostility that began between the two groups when Liberia came into being in 1822. Most disastrously, the continued animosity occasionally led to violent incidents; the most serious took place in 1980 when the Liberian army vanquished the NTWP-led government.

The discussion up to this juncture illustrates that despite its various forms, the political development of Liberia from 1822 to the twentieth century was dominated by the practice of power centralization. While the pressures created by the indigenous Africans and the European powers played an enhancing role in this development, the ACS was its main formulator and reinforcer. As has been demonstrated throughout this chapter, the continuation of the practice did not mean that it was not opposed. The irregular, militant opposition to it from 1822 until 1980 bears testimony to this. Doubtless, such opposition was principally caused by the failure of the practice to accommodate politically a large number of people it claimed it represented. As will be examined in the next chapter, the economic formation of Liberia as an integral part of the overall institutional formation of that country contributed to the continuation of the described political development, and, of course, its deficiencies and blunders.

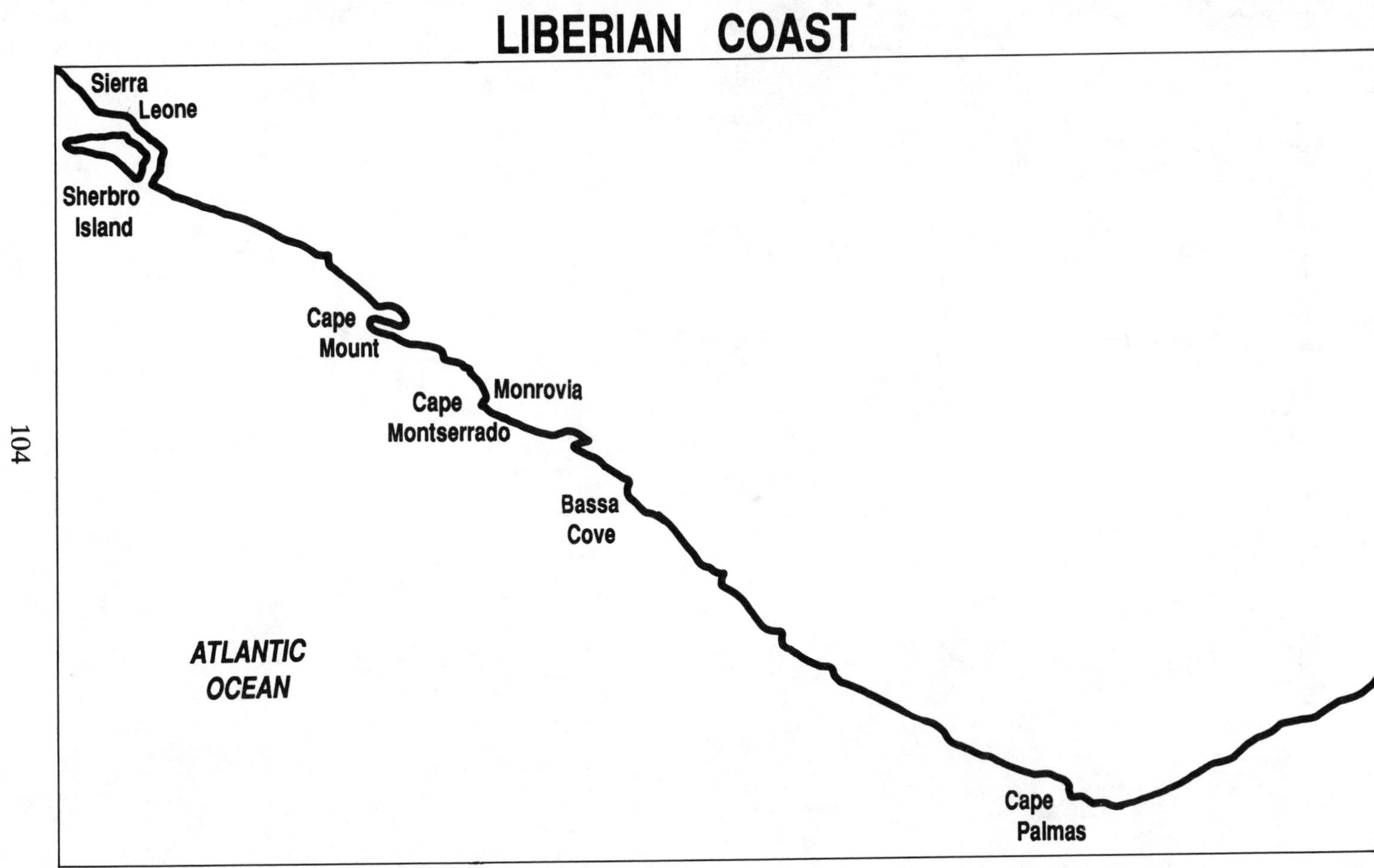
LIBERIAN COAST
Sierra Leone
Sherbro Island
Cape Mount
Cape Montserrado
Monrovia
Bassa Cove
Cape Palmas
ATLANTIC OCEAN

NOTES

Chapter IV

[1]For the details of this definition, see the following works: Maurice Cornforth, *Historical Maternalism* (New York, 1977), pp. 96-109; Genovese, *The World the Slaveholders Made*, pp. 126-150; W. J. Cash, *The Mind of the South* (New York, 1960), pp. 8, 10, 48, 61-62; Merle Curties, *The Social Ideas of American Educators* (New York, 1935); Richard Hofstadter, *Social Darwinism in American Thought* (Boston, 1967); Winthrope Jordan, *The Whiteman's Burden: Historical Origins of Racism* (New York, 1978); Eugene Kamenka, *Marxism and Ethics* (London, 1970); Ernest Mandel and George Novack, *The Marxist Theory of Alienation* (New York, 1976); M. I. Finley, *Ancient Slavery and Modern Ideology* New York, 1980); Herbert Aptheker, *The Nature of Democracy, Freedom, and Revolution* (New York, 1975).

[2]West, *Back to Africa*, p. 107.

[3]Quoted in *Ibid*; see also Charles H. Huberich, *The Political and Legislative History of Liberia*, Vol. I (New York, 1947), pp. 80-81.

[4]The following works testify to this: Genovese, *Roll Jordan Roll*; Genovese, *The World the Slaveholders Made*; Jordan, *White Over Black*; Oakes, *The Ruling Race*; Litwack, *North of Slavery*; and Fitzhugh, *The Sociology of the South*.

[5]J. Ashmun, *Memoir . . . of the Rev. Samuel Bacon* (Washington, 1822), p. 253; West, *Back to Africa*, p. 108.

[6]Huberich, *Political and Legislative History*, Vol. I, pp. 94, 95, 156, 157 and 182.

[7]Gurley, *Life of Ashmun*, p. 129.

[8]West, *Back to Africa*, p. 126.

[9]*Ibid.*, pp. 125-130.

[10]*Ibid.*, p. 126.

[11]*Ibid.*, p. 127; see also Gurley, *Life of Ashmun*.

[12]Monrovia, the town that became the chief city of Liberia, was planned by the founders of the ACS who viewed it as an "extension" of America to Africa.

[13]West, *Back to Africa*, p. 127.

[14]*Ibid.*, p. 128; and Gurley, *Life of Ashmun*, pp. 190-192.

[15]Gurley, *Life of Ashmun*, p. 191.

[16]West, *Back to Africa*, p. 128.

[17]Gurley, *Life of Ashmun*, pp. 190-193.

[18]West, *Back to Africa*, p. 128.

[19]*Ibid.*

[20]For the details of this meeting, see Gurley's *Life of Ashmun*.

[21]*Ibid.*

[22]*African Repository*, I (1824), p. 24; West, *Back to Africa*, p. 130.

[23]*African Repository*, I (1824), p. 24.

[24]Although this is not clearly spelled out in surviving accounts, the description provided seems to sustain what really happened. For details of this see: West, *Back to Africa*, pp. 129-131.

[25]*African Repository*, II (1825), p. 25; West, *Back to Africa*, p. 131.

[26]*Ibid.*

[27]Besides providing living accommodation, the house also represented a symbol of supreme authority. No wonder it was the best house in the colony.

[28]West, *Back to Africa*, p. 132.

[29]*Constitution, Government, and Digest of the Laws of Liberia as Confirmed and Established by the Board of Managers of the American Colonization Society* (Washington, 1825), pp. 3-7.

[30]This provision was mainly designed against Carey who had used his religious influence to rally the settlers against Ashmun. Anon., "Review on African Colonization," *The Quarterly Christian Spectator*, II (1830), p. 468; Fox, *American Colonization Society; The Baptist General Convention, Fifth Triennial Proceedings* (1826), pp. 20-21; George D. Brown, "History of Protestant Episcopal Mission in Liberia Up to 1838," *Magazine of the Protestant Episcopal Church*, 39 (1970); Forster, "Colonization of Free Negroes in Liberia, 1816-1835", p. 53; and *The Constitution, Government, and Digest of Laws of Liberia*, pp. 9-11.

[31]Forster, "Colonization of Free Negroes in Liberia, 1816-1835," p. 53.

[32]*Twelfth Annual Report of the ACS* (Washington, 1828), pp. 35-36.

[33]Gurley, *Life of Ashmun*, p. 251.

[34]West, *Back to Africa*, p. 130.

[35]*Ibid*, pp. 128-130.

[36]See note 4.

[37]Maugham, *The Republic of Liberia*, pp. 82-83.

[38]See note 4.

[39]Huberich, *Political and Legislative History*, Vol. I, pp. 752-753.

[40]West, *Back to Africa*, pp. 151-152.

[41]See the following works for this misleading argument: *Ibid*; Dories Henries, *The Liberian Nation: A Short History* (New York, 1954); George W. Ellis, *Negro Culture in West Africa* (New York, 1915); and Joseph J. Roberts, *The Republic of Liberia* (Washington, 1869).

[42]Shick, *Behold the Promised Land*, p. 45; Luther P. Jackson, *Free Negro Labor and Property Holding in Virginia, 1830-1860* (New York, 1942), p. 20; and Luther P. Jackson, "Free Negroes of Petersburg, Virginia," *Journal of Negro History*, 12 (1927), pp. 373-375.

[43]Jackson, "Free Negroes of Petersburg," pp. 373-375.

[44]West, *Back to Africa*, p. 152.

[45]John Cummings, *Negro Population in the United States, 1790-1915* (Washington, 1918), p. 210; Leon Litwack, *North of Slavery: The Negro in the Free States, 1790-1860* (Chicago, 1961), pp. 182-186; and J. W. Wilson, *Sketches of the Higher Classes of Colored Society in Philadelphia* (Philadelphia, 1841), pp. 47-97.

[46]*Ibid*; M. H. Freeman, "The Education Wants of the Free Colored People," *Anglo-African Magazine*, I (1858), pp. 116-119; Berlin, *Slaves Without Masters*, pp. 195-199, 246-249.

[47]Berlin, *Slaves Without Masters*, pp. 215-216.

[48]See note 41.

[49]J. B. Webster and A. A. Boahen, *The Revolutionary Years: West Africa Since 1800* (London, 1980), p. 128.

[50]*Ibid.*, pp. 124-125 and 128.

[51]This charge was influenced by the fact that the governor showed more favoritism toward the Baptist Church than the Methodist Episcopal.

[52]George Brown, *The Economic History of Liberia* (Washington, 1941), p. 122.

[53]*Ibid.*, p. 242.

[54]*Ibid.*, pp. 242-243.

[55]Quoted in Shick, *Behold the Promised Land*, p. 40.

[56]See note 54.

[57]Commonwealth Legislative Minutes, 1839-1849, Liberian National Archives (Monrovia).

[58]For the details of this, see: Penelope Campbell, *Maryland in Africa: The Maryland Colonization Society, 1831-1867* (Urbana, 1971).

[59]Brown, *Economic History*, p. 129.

[60]*Ibid.*

[61]Quoted in Huberich, *Political and Legislative History*, Vol. I, p. 774.

[62]Yancy, *Historical Light of Liberia*, p. 54.

[63]Brown, *Economic History*, p. 130.

[64]*Ibid.*

[65]*Ibid.*

[66]Raymond L. Buell, *The Native Problem in Africa*, Vol. 2 (New York, 1928), pp. 706-707.

[67]Brown, *Economic History*, p. 130.

[68]McPherson,*A History of Liberia*, p. 29.

[69]Brown, *Economic History*, p. 130.

[70]Yancy, *Historical Light of Liberia*, p. 57.

[71]Republic of Liberia, *The Declaration of Independence of Liberia* (Monrovia, 1847).

[72]I have refused to use the word *new* because, as is illustrated in the body of this chapter, Liberia did not, although it declared its independence on July 26, 1847, get rid of the institutional values it inherited form the ACS.

[73]Yancy, *Historical Light of Liberia*, p. 57.

[74]*Ibid*., pp. 58-60.

[75]Republic of Liberia, *The Declaration of Independence*.

[76]The American Declaration of Independence was, however, mainly framed as a protest to the wrongs done to America by Britain.

[77]Republic of Liberia, *Constitution of the Republic of Liberia* (Monrovia, 1847); Sidney De La Rue, *The Land of the Pepper Bird* (New York, 1930), p. 219.

[78]A. Karnga,*A Guide to Our Criminal and Civil Procedure* (Liverpool, 1926), p. 45; _______, *History of Liberia* (London, 1927).

[79]Commonwealth Legislative Minutes, 1837-1847.

[80]Webster and Boahen, *The Revolutionary Years*, pp. 127-128.

[81]Karnga, *History of Liberia,* pp. 45-46.

[82]*African Repository*, XXIV (1848), pp. 120-126.

[83]*Ibid.*, XXVIII (1852),p. 137.

[84]*Ibid.*, XXVII (1851), p. 120.

[85]From J. J. Roberts to the Liberian Senate and House of Representatives in *Ibid.*, pp. 120-121.

[86]The area was bought with a sum of 2,000 pounds. For the details of this see West, *Back to Africa*, pp. 224-225.

[87]*Ibid.*, p. 225. Indeed, at the zenith of the Europeans' dismembermentof Africa, about half of Liberia was taken by the British and French. Webster and Boahen, *The Revolutionary Years*, p. 127.

[88]For details of this, see The Republic of Liberia, *Treaties and Conventions Concluded Between Liberia and Foreign Powers, 1847-1907* (Monrovia, 1907).

[89]*African Repository*, XL (1864), p. 108.

[90]*Ibid.*, XLIV (1868), p. 134-144.

[91]The True Whig National Convention (1869), Liberian National Archives (Monrovia).

[92]Karnga, *History of Liberia*, pp. 140-146.

[93]The True Whig National Convention.

[94]*Ibid.*

[95]*African Repository*, XLVI (1870), pp. 102-111.

[96]*Ibid.*, p. 106. As new initiatives, President Roye proposed an efficient national banking system and other developments such as an educational system that would incorporate the indigenous Africans. This idea was encouraged by Edward W. Blyden, a prominent Whig who favored the accommodation of the indigenous Africans. Of course, this was in line with his African nationalism. For the details of the above argument, see Lynch's *Edward Wilmont Blyden.*

[97]While some have argued that President Roye's death was caused by his attackers, other have maintained that he was drowned as he tried to escape with money he had stolen from the Liberian people.

[98]This was enhanced by the fact that, although he won the presidential election in 1869, Roye "inherited a civil service" that was dominated by the mulattoes. For the details of this, see Webster and Boahen, *The Revolutionary Years*, pp. 128-129.

[99]*Ibid.*

[100]Joseph E. Holloway, *Liberian Diplomacy in Africa: A Study in Inter-African Relations* (Washington, 1981), pp. 153-161.

[101]Webster and Boahen, *The Revolutionary Years*, pp. 130-136.

[102]This has been thoroughly treated in Martin Lowenkopf, *Politics in Liberia: The Conservative Road to Development* (Stanford, 1976).

CHAPTER V

THE AMERICAN COLONIZATION SOCIETY AND THE DEVELOPMENT OF ECONOMIC INSTITUTIONS IN LIBERIA

Like the other main institutional developments of Liberia, the economic formation of that country was profoundly influenced by the ACS. Since the ACS was functionally paternalistic, it influenced paternalistically nearly all Liberia's institutional developments.[1] No doubt, this trend was enhanced by the social stratification that had been introduced on the pre-Liberian coast by the world economic system and the advance of that system in what became Liberia. Such factors were to reinforce the ACS' system of paternalism. Paternalism and its reinforcers were to call into being an economic formation in Liberia that was characteristically and structurally dependent, or was incapable of expanding on its own.[2] Although it was largely established and promoted by the ACS, Liberia's economic dependency increasingly became conditioned and determined by the nineteenth century world economic system. This should not be surprising for, as will be illustrated, the institutional values introduced in Liberia by the ACS did not radically differ from those inherent in the world economic system.

The history of the development of dependent economic institutions in Liberia began immediately after the first group of black Americans and their white leaders landed at the area that became Liberia in 1822. This development took hold of the American settlers because, as they were being sent to West Africa, they were made to rely solely on the ACS for leadership and material support. Their dependence on the ACS was further reinforced when the Liberian colony was established. They consistently called on the ACS for almost every basic necessity after their arrival in West Africa. Items often requested and received included tobacco, rice, flour, bacon, guns, and gunpowder, cloth, and building materials.[3] By 1826, Liberia's first newspaper, the *Liberian Herald*, published a notice that certain settlers wanted these items:

> . . . boards, planks, shingles, window glass, nails, crockery, all kinds of hardware, household furniture, cutlery, tobacco, pipes, . . . American cottons, ginghams, calicoes, shoes, hose, cambrics, muslims, linens, buttons, thread, combs, butter, lard and hams. In exchange for which may be . . . camwood, ivory, turtle shells, gold dust, deer, leopard, and tiger skins, rice, fowl, fish, goats, sheep, and fruit.[4]

Work on Ashmun's house had been delayed because of the late arrival of boards and other construction materials from the United States.[5] This was a further indication that Liberia was from the start a dependent colony.

Reliance on supplies from the ACS was only one aspect of this economic relationship of dependency. Another was reliance on the indigenous Africans for tropical products that the settlers needed for the international trade. It was against this background that Ashmun decided to establish a permanent commercial venture between the settlers and the Africans. Ashmun's attempt, however, was opposed by the Africans on the grounds that they had not received fair prices for their products; but their united stand was not to last long. Personal interest evidently undermined group solidarity. Chief Bromley, who was one of the leaders of the Africans, informed Ashmun in 1823, for example, that he would continue to be a friend of the settlers. He later added that he was prepared to sell them a large quantity of rice. He was to use his tremendous influence to persuade the nearby African chiefs to resolve their grievances with the American settlers. He further requested Ashmun to discuss issues of mutual interest.[6]

With these cordial gestures, the settlers decided to react in kind. Trade between them and the Africans was intensified in 1823. Ashmun quickly recognized the importance of this and,therefore, recommended the building of trading outposts on the coast east of the Liberian settlement. He correctly reasoned that such trading centers would enhance the buying of African goods.[7]

Having recognized the significance of trading with the Africans, Ashmun decided to appeal to the ACS for goods that would be exchanged for locally produced African goods. The items requested included tobacco, whiskey, silks, guns, gunpowder, knives, and pipes. To win the support of the ACS for his request, Ashmun informed that body that a large vessel was being built in the settlement that would transport 250 bushels of rice or four tons of wood with ease between the coastal area from Cape Palmas and Sierra Leone. According to him, the vessel would be manned by only four persons, and it would "command all the trades . . . ," and then "save to the friends of the colony thousands of dollars annually."[8]

As the settlement matured, the role of the settlers as middlemen between the Africans and overseas traders, not just the ACS, was reinforced. This development was partially encouraged by the fact that the soil around the immediate environs of Monrovia was poor for agricultural activities. Added to this was the failure of the settlers to develop a taste for African crops such as cassava, plantains, and yams. Although some kept livestock for home consumption, most settlers initially became artisans or traders, since these vocations brought them quick profits. Those who turned to commercial ventures bought American cloth, rum, tobacco, etc., and exchanged them for African products that were demanded by both the local and international markets.[9]

Seeing the danger of the settlers' increasing reliance on the Africans, Ashmun warned the former of it in 1823:

> The cultivation of your rich land is the only way you will ever find out to independence, comfort and wealth. . . . If agriculture is neglected . . . you must send to America for every article of provisions. . . . Suppose however, the natives should do what they have often done already--prohibit all intercourse with you. . . . The moment they find you are depending on them, they . . . make you pay four or five prices for everything they sell to you. . . . Are you so lost to all senses of shame, as to be willing to depend on half a naked savage to feed you?[10]

Besides, Ashmun admonished them that the middleman role they played between the Africans and the foreign traders could never bring wealth to the colony. He therefore advised them to grow their own bananas, oranges, guava, paw-paw, and pineapple.[11]

These warnings did not, however, stop the settlers from serving as middlemen. Besides the reasons already given there were other factors that ensured the intensification of this role. The settlers did not have the means to displace the Africans who controlled the interior trade. This could also be said about their relationship with the western traders who dominated the overseas trade. This meant that the settlers had little choice but to cooperate with both the Africans and the traders. This trend was reinforced by the following factors: capital and western goods which were increasingly demanded by the settlers were too scarce in the settlement. Added to this was the inability of the settlers to produce the goods needed for the overseas trade, and of the ACS to provide the kind of capital resources which would have made the settlers independent producers or allowed them to make effective use of the land and the labor force of the colony. It is not, therefore, surprising that even a man like Ashmun, who had cautioned the settlers against relying heavily on commerce, was to become a trader himself.[12]

It was against this background that a merchant class began to emerge in Liberia after 1822. Indeed, by 1828, this class was able to satisfy both the internal and external commercial needs of the settlement. But this development reinforced the social stratifications that had already been introduced on the coast of pre-Liberia by the Atlantic slave trade.[13] Every settler's family, especially the ones with some property, employed from one to four indigenous Africans at the average cost of about $4.00 to $6.00 a month.[14] This practice was later extended to include the father and son-like value that was inherent in paternalism. A clear demonstration came in 1822 when Jack Ben, an African chief, decided to send his son to a settler's family to be westernized. In return for his training, the child was requested to do domestic work for the family. Indeed, many African children were to receive their western training in the settlement in this way. Adult Africans who later became involved with the practice were required to perform services on settlers' farms. This kind of master and servant relationship led the settlers to view the Africans as a "peon class," and themselves as a ruling class.[15]

As the colony grew and its trade became internationally oriented, the ruling class came increasingly to be dominated by the most wealthy individuals. Between 1822 and 1828, Carey, one of the most influential men in the colony, shipped about 6,000 pounds of coffee to Richmond, Virginia.[16] Frances Devancy, another eminent settler, testified that through trade in the colony, he accumulated wealth valued at about $20,000. Some eight settler ships were involved with the trade that linked the settlement with the outside world. Their exports included: dyewood, hide, ivory, gold, rice, and palm oil. These were exchanged for European and American cloth, tobacco, and arms. From the beginning of 1826 to the middle of that year, Liberia exported about $30,786 worth of African products.[17]

As such economic activities brought some benefits to Liberia they were increasingly challenged. The eight Liberian ships involved with the trade were later rivalled, for example, by eight American vessels. The latter's net export to Liberia in 1829 amounted to $20,000. By 1832, foreign vessels from the following countries called at Liberia's ports: 32 from America, 22 from Britain, and 2 from France. The goods brought by these vessels were valued at $125,549.[18] Indeed, less than a decade later, Liberia's net imports far outweighted its net exports. While it imported $157,829 worth of goods in 1843, the colony exported less than half that amount in the same year. The items imported included dried fish, flour, beef, butter, coffee, bread, cornmeal, vinegar, molasses, ham, bacon, tobacco, cigars, sugar, soap, candles, cloth, guns, gunpowder, and rum.[19] These items were exchanged for African products which money value was far less than that of the goods imported.[20]

Obviously, Liberia's trade deficit was a direct result of what some contemporary scholars have termed "unequal exchange."[21] It is fair to maintain, however, that the ascendency of this mode of exchange in Liberia was enhanced by the various values of the elites of the settlement. As noted, the failure of the elites to develop appetites for goods produced locally forced them to depend increasingly on imported products. While the foregoing consumption pattern was associated with social prestige, it drained the scarce resources of the settlement.[22] This was more so, since the goods imported were more expensive than the ones exported. Added to this was the fact that the imported goods were not ones which could bring about a self-sustaining economic development. They were mostly consumable items.[23]

Liberia's emerging trading system was thus to reinforce the dependent tendency inherent in the paternalistic political culture that was introduced in that country by the ACS. This was already apparent by the middle of the nineteenth century. It was not altered by increasing exports of agricultural produce from settler farms nor by the increasing export of palm kernels. The latter would be a tropical product in increasing demand by European industrialists in the nineteenth century,[24] but the supply of palm kernels for the world market merely reinforced rather than altered the pattern of dependency.

The foregoing commercial ventures, however, did bring wealth to certain Liberians by the 1850s. These included General A. Sherman, Roberts, Roye, John Russwurm, Buchanan, Yates, Payne, Benson, Warner, and Newport, all of whom were members of the elite class. General Sherman, for example, was said to be among the richest of the elites. He owned fifteen vessels and possessed the most beautiful building in Monrovia at the time. His commercial relationships with the outside world included traders in the United States, Germany, France, and Britain.[25]

As already indicated in Chapter Four, many among the elites began to dominate political developments in Liberia. This started in the early history of the country. Carey and Ashmun were traders and also eminent leaders in the settlement. The influence of the commercial class was predominant in the Colonial Council. Like nearly all the top political and other social positions of pre-independent Liberia, people from the commerical class occupied those of independent Liberia. Indeed, the most wealthy of the merchant class were to be aristocratically ordained the "merchant princes." Eight of the eleven members of the Council were, for example, from this group in 1840.[26] Before he became president, Warner, who was then a successful merchant, clearly spelled out, in 1850, the relationship between political and commercial developments in pre- and post-independent Liberia in these terms: "You ought not to be surprised to find us first in the Government and then in the shipyard--this is necessary to raise and build Liberia."[27]

Doubtless, their political supremacy, as that of their economic domination, was challenged. Unlike the former, which was primarily threatened by internal pressures, the latter was challenged by forces that were largely external. As mentioned before, the external threats to their commercial gains came from the European powers, especially British traders who were based in Sierra Leone. In fact, European commercial activities on the coast of West Africa had been clearly evident long before Liberia was established. Indeed, when Liberia was founded the British already had trading outposts in close proximity to that colony.[28] The establishment of the Liberian colony was interpreted by these traders as a serious threat to their commercial interests. This was reinforced as the Liberian colony began to expand its influence over the nearby indigenous Africans with whom the British traders dealt on the coast of West Africa.[29]

Because of this fear, British traders decided to appeal to their government for assistance, a request that was occasionally honored.[30] With this support, the Sierra Leone-based British traders frequently ignored the commercial interests of Liberia on the ground that the settlement was not a sovereign entity. But this action and the rationale for it precipitated an immediate reaction from the authorities of Liberia. As noted before, the desire to affirm Liberia's sovereignty became the supreme objective of the leaders of that country.

Evidently, therefore, this desire was more economic than political. This is further substantiated by the fact that most legislative bills passed in early independent Liberia were designed to bring the coastal trade under the control of the leaders of that country. In 1849, an act known as the Regulating Navigation, Commerce, and Revenue Act was passed. In later years, the Republicans enacted similar bills including a bill that circumscribed foreign traders to only six Liberian ports. One of the bills also stipulated that foreign traders could trade only through Liberian merchants. This was mainly designed to protect the intermediary role the latter already played between the indigenous Africans and the European traders.[31]

The attempts to arrest the commercial activities of British traders brought about a counterreaction from that group. A British trading firm which had contacts with the coast of Liberia before 1847 unsuccessfully tried to appeal to the British government not to recognize the independence of that country.[32] The owners of the firm rightly reasoned that if Britain recognized the independence of Liberia, their rationale for transgressing the commercial interests of that colony would become baseless. In 1849, the same firm informed the British Foreign Office of its opposition to the rights Liberia assumed over the area where it conducted trade. The owners of the firm warned the British Foreign Office that if they were forced to leave the Liberian coast, "American traders were ready to fill the void."[33]

Despite these warnings, the British government failed to employ measures that would completely undermine the commercial interest of the Liberian elites. There were several reasons for British reaction to the winnings. First, this was not what the British trading interests in Sierra Leone specifically requested. They merely wanted Liberia to relax the various newly passed bills that affected their commercial activities on the coastal area of that country. Second, although it passed these restrictive bills, Liberia was unable to enforce them effectively. This was largely due to the fact that it did not have the naval power to put them in force along its vast coastal area.[34] With this, the British traders in Sierra Leone continued successfully to penetrate the very market the bills were designed to protect. This success, however, further indicated that the restrictive bills were not as rigid as the British traders had labeled them. No wonder the British government continued to give only sporadic attention to the series of calls made by its traders concerning the bills up to the 1860s.[35]

There was one other reason why the British government responded to the bills as it did. In 1848, Liberia signed a commercial treaty with Britain which favored the British. By the terms of the treaty, the two countries agreed that a perpetual peace should exist between them. The agreement also stipulated that: "citizens of Britain could reside and trade in any part of (Liberia) without being restrained or prejudiced by any monopoly . . . or exclusive privilege of sale or purchase whatever. . . ."[36] Although it allowed British traders to trade with any Liberian, the treaty maintained that this was to be monitored by the Liberian authorities. This aspect of the treaty was, however, later modified to be more auspicious for Britain. Through its Consul, A. W. Hanson, who resided in Monrovia, Britain pressured Liberia to make the following provisions: that British citizens be unconditionally allowed to trade with anyone they wanted in Liberia; and that the property rights

British citizens had in Liberia before independence be restored. Liberia was not only asked to open its doors to all the commercial powers, but it was also told to allow the citizens of such powers to establish factories in any part of Liberia they pleased. Liberia's duty on an imported good was not to exceed five percent of the cost of the goods. The Consul advised Liberia that if these mandates were accepted, that country would grow economically.[37]

Consul Hanson probably did not have to make the final appeal to influence Liberia to comply. All the mandates came directly from Viscount Palmerston, the British Secretary of State for Foreign Affairs, and Liberia's President Roberts was aware of the fact that the edicts were backed by the Britsh navy.[38] Having no navy to match that of the British, President Roberts decided to appease the British in this way:

> Our consideration will be given to your several suggestions and propositions; and that the legislature entertains the most lively disposition to meet the wishes of her Majesty's Government in all matters connected with Her Majesty's subjects' interests in trade of this coast.[39]

No doubt, this kind of response to the Britsh government influenced it not to take drastic measures against Liberia despite the fact that the African republic did not always implement what it had accepted and promised.[40]

President Robert's strategy was also employed to counterpoise other foreign traders who were active on the Liberian coast. In 1852, he signed a treaty of commerce and navigation with Louis Napoleon Bonaparte, the President of the French Republic. Its contents were the same as the one signed between Liberia and Britain.[41] Indeed, Liberia later signed similar treaties with Belgium, the Netherlands, Denmark, Italy, Sweden, Norway, Spain, Portugal, Haiti, the United States, and the confederate states of Germany. These treaties stipulated that their signers were not to transgress the sovereign rights of each other.[42]

While these treaties helped to discourage the Europeans from directly taking over the commerce of Liberia, they also reinforced the middleman role that country's elites already played between the indigenous Africans and the foreign traders. As noted before, this had begun in the early history of Liberia when settlers with capital had bought African products such as palm oil, rice, camwood, etc., and had sold them to their foreign counterparts on the coast. Although it was occasionally disrupted, sometimes by wars between the settlers and the Africans, and other times by harsh climatic conditions or foreign competitors, the middleman role increasingly became an integral part of the merchant class mode of production. Indeed, this role succeeded in bringing tremendous wealth to a few members of the merchant class. This was clearly illustrated by the number of vessels owned and operated by certain members of the foregoing class. From 1847 to 1870, they owned 139 commercial vessels. Although most of them were limited to the coastal area between Sierra Leone and what became Nigeria, some of the ships carried goods as far as Europe and the United States.[43]

But their success was to give way to a new economic and less optimistic reality. Doubtless, this was caused by factors that were largely external. The demand for Liberian camwood, palm kernels, and palm oil by foreign markets declined. The decline was due to the introduction of other products such as "aniline dyes" and oils that were superior to camwood, or palm oil.[44] The drop in demand for Liberia's palm oil was noted in 1873 when an unidentified Liberian remarked that the price of Liberia's palm oil was declining as a result of foreign competition. One J. M. Turner made a similar emphasis in the same year when he put forward that the "fluctuation of foreign markets meant that Liberian oil was gradually losing its character as a profitable commodity."[45]

With this fall in demand, it is not surprising that the same decade witnessed serious problems for Liberian merchant firms.[46] This was reflected, among other things, by a decline in the size of Liberia's merchant marine. This was composed of 137 operational vessels in 1870, but it dramatically shrunk to 29 in 1872. By 1882, it was reduced to 14 vessels. By the end of 1883, Liberia had fewer than four operational vessels.[47]

In addition to commerce, agricultural activities, especially the ones associated with exportable crops, also brought wealth to certain members of the elite class. This was especially so for those who took up land along the St. Paul River and in Bassa County.[48] From the 1850s to 1865, large sugar and coffee plantations were developed in these areas, principally in the area that became commonly known as Upriver. This was enhanced by the fact that the land in that area was fertile and labor easily obtainable.[49] As early as 1842, Reverend Wilson and Cyrus Willi, who were both Upriver planters, declared that they were prepared to produce several thousand pounds of sugar. In 1848, moreover, Willi managed to produce three thousand pounds of sugar.[50] This was not at all unusual as another Upriver planter, Abraham Blackledge, maintained in 1851 that he sold "four thousand pounds" of sugar. He anticipated even greater production in the form of "ten thousand pounds and between eight and nine hundred gallons of syrup."[51]

These were not isolated or unusual examples of success in sugar production. W. S. Anderson, another successful Upriver planter, estimated that about seventy thousand pounds of sugar were exported in 1863. The United States received fifty thousand pounds of the above amount. The remainder was exported to Sierra Leone and other settlements along the West African coast.[52]

Like Liberia's camwood and palm oil industries, however, the sugar was decreasingly demanded by the external markets. This was dictated by several factors. During the American Civil War, the main home source of America's sugar supply, the South, was disrupted. This created a demand for Liberia's sugar. The demand ceased, however, two years after the war ended. Cuba's emergence as America's key supplier also ensured the decline in demand for Liberia's sugar. By 1877, for example, the United States received eighty-two per cent of the net sugar export of Cuba.[53]

Liberia's coffee experienced the same fate as its sugar. Coffee was among the first group of crops exported from Liberia. Indeed, from 1828 to the 1850s, coffee was among Liberia's most important export crops.[54] It brought tremendous wealth to Carey and a few other Liberian coffee planters. Thus by the early 1860s, there were about 46,649 newly growing coffee trees in the Upriver area.[55]

Like its sugar, camwood, and palm oil businesses, nevertheless, Liberia's coffee production was largely undermined by external pressures. The decline of coffee production began in the 1880s. Some twenty years earlier, young coffee trees from Liberia had been shipped to Brazil, Guadeloupe, and other parts of the West Indies where they had been successfully cultivated. This experiment was an alternative to the native coffee plants of those regions which were increasingly being destroyed by a colorless worm.[56] As it turned out, the auspicious tilling of the new coffee plants in those areas actually played a key role in the collapse of Liberia's overseas export coffee business. As coffee cultivation prospered in Brazil and the West Indies, the United States, which was Liberia's main coffee buyer, decided to turn to the former, especially to Brazil, which finally succeeded in monopolizing the coffee market of the United States.[57] It is not, therefore, surprising that Liberia's coffee exports to the United States came to a complete halt by the 1880s. This only worsened Liberia's already deteriorating commercial position as its national economy had come to rely heavily on coffee exports to America.[58]

Moreover, Liberia was not able to make up for this loss through sales to Europe. In the early 1890s, Liberia exported 980,847 pounds of coffee to Europe; but by 1900, this amount was reduced to "a half million pounds" per year.[59] At about the same time, there was an additional drop in the price of Liberian palm oil largely due to the discovery and use of petroleum products in the United States and Europe.[60]

Besides these factors, other external pressures also speeded up Liberia's commercial failure. By the end of the nineteenth century, European merchants with their efficient steamships had succeeded in removing the old fashioned ships of the Liberian "merchant princes" from the oceans. This corresponded with the active presence of European traders in Liberia itself. Among the most active were traders from Germany. The fact that the colonies of Germany were unable to provide all that country's tropical wants caused German traders to involve themselves increasingly with the commerce of Liberia.[61] In fact, they had taken the lead in competition for the Liberian market by 1900. Germans owned, for example, two of every three ships that sailed to Liberia around the turn of the century; accordingly, Germany received the greatest portion of that country's trade.[62] The Hamburg based firm, G. Woerwaum and Company, had the largest commercial firm in Liberia. This included "wholesale and retail stores" which were established in Liberia's main seaports such as Monrovia, Harper, Buchanan, Cestos, and Robertsport.[63] German commercial ventures also extended to the interior of Liberia.[64] By the 1900s, some twenty-six German firms were operating in Monrovia. Herr Dirklage, who was one of the managers of these companies also served as Liberia's Consul in Hamburg, Germany.[65] Other foreign firms in Liberia included those from Britain, Holland and Belgium.[66]

The commercial advances of these foreign firms actually reduced Liberia's "merchant princes" to little more than petty traders by the end of the nineteenth century. This was heightened by the fact that the European merchants who now controlled the commerce of Liberia preferred giving key commercial responsibilities to people from their own counties rather than to Liberian citizens.[67] Indeed, with one exception, the Liberian traders whose ancestors once owned nearly all the businesses of their country after the turn of the century were servants of the various European firms that had taken over Liberia's commerce.[68]

It is evident, therefore, that the many legislative enactments passed to arrest the commercial advance of Europeans in Liberia did not succeed in accomplishing that objective. Liberia's "merchant princes" could not possibly withstand the challenge posed to them by the European traders.[69] This was not likely to occur since their trading relationship with the Europeans continued to reinforce the historical process that ensured their inherited role as dependent and unequal partners. Obviously, this was a logical outcome of the nature of the relationship itself. The European traders were directly associated with the countries which owned the financial institutions and contolled the markets of the world, and this meant that they were in a better position than their Liberian counterparts to determine that relationship on their behalf.[70] Therefore, it is not surprising that they succeeded in superseding the "merchant princes" before 1900.

This did not mean, however, that the relationship did not bring any rewards to the Liberian merchant class. Indeed, this kind of commercial relationship usually exists between countries or among countries when mutual benefits are being realized by the merchant classes or elites of the countries involved.[71] The fact that most of the Liberian elites during the period under study acquired their status through commerce bears testimony to this argument. But as mentioned, the wealth procured from that specialized function was relatively insubstantial and, above all, too economically unproductive to have accommodated a large number of the Liberian people. This was especially so, since the assets obtained were mostly not capital goods. This, together with the group's consuming pattern, which attached great value to foreign items, left little capital for a self-sustaining economic initiative.[72]

As noted in Chapter Four, Liberia experienced more than economic subordination in the last half of the nineteenth century; its sovereignty was also transgressed during the same period. In 1885, Britain pressured Liberia to sign a border treaty.[73] The treaty, commonly known as the Blyden-Havelock Treaty, allowed Britain to take over the Gallinas territory which Liberia had bought in 1848.[74] Indeed sixty miles of its southwestern coastal line were allotted to Britain by the treaty. In return, Britain offered $7,075 to Liberia for the area that was said to have been valued at about $100,000.[75]

Six years after this treaty, France, which already had a colony southeast of Liberia, decided to make similar territorial claims. It maintained that its border should be stretched some ninety miles into Liberia. Despite the fact that Liberia appealed to all the great powers, including the United States, to discourage France from executing the claim, the French pressured Liberia to accept the territorial loss in 1897. In return, Liberia received a compensation of 25,000 francs for this territory, which was more than a third of the country's original size (see map p. 148).[76]

As Europeans encroached on their country and commerce, the Liberian elites were forced to make increasing demands for the labor forces of the indigenous Africans and the recaptives. As noted, the beginning of this development could be traced back to the early history of Liberia. As early as 1822, indigenous African children had been employed to do domestic work for the settlers in exchange for receiving a western education. Indigenous adult Africans who showed friendly attitudes toward the settlers were asked to perform service on "large gardens" and later on farms of the latter in exchange for western goods.[77] In fact, nearly all the large sugar and coffee plantations that were developed in Liberia were worked almost entirely either by the Africans or the recaptives.[78]

Various nineteenth century reports and accounts of Liberia give evidence of this situation. It was noted in the 1890s, for example, that most of the settlers depended on the Africans for labor.[79] Governor John B. Pinney (1822-1835) put forward in 1834 that "nothing had heretofore been done for the natives, except to educate a few . . . in the capacity of servants."[80] Elder S. S. Ball, who visited Liberia in 1848, observed that indigenous Africans were "bound" to the settlers "for a term of years under what is called the apprentice system." Ball also maintained that almost every well-to-do settler in Monrovia had from ten to fifteen African servants.[81] Matilda R. Lomax, a settler, wrote to a friend in the United States arguing that "labourers can be hired in Liberia for twenty-five cents per day--and at the outside from three to four dollars per month; a person may hire good common labourers to work the ground to make it productive as in the States comparatively speaking. . . ."[83] Lieutenant Bridge of the United States Navy wrote in 1848 that "buggies" were used by the Africans to transport both missionaries and settlers in Monrovia.[84]

It is thus clear that the settlers came quickly to rely heavily on African labor. Anderson, the prosperous settler sugar planter, explained the reliance on the Africans and recaptives in these terms:

> My entire family operations are carried with them (Congoes and some few Golas). My steam mill has for its engineer a Vai boy. My sugar-maker . . . and fireman are Congoes and their entire acquaintance with the material parts have gained by observation. At wood chopping they cannot be excelled. Seven boys or young men have in three weeks time cut one hundred and seventy five cords of wood, and when I tell you how they managed thus to do, it will be another fact to prove that the hope of reward (for) labour. These boys are my apprentices, and they cut each as his week's work five cords of wood and put it up; for all they cut and put up over that quantity, I pay them fifty cents per cord.[85]

This use of African labor was to lead to accusations that the settlers were employing them in a way that was not different from slavery. Stebbins, a strong critic of the colonization initiative, charged that in 1837, John N. Lewis, who was the Secretary of the ACS in Liberia, served as a "storekeeper" in Monrovia for Pedro Blanco, a Spanish slaver who had a trading station in Gallinas. The charge was brought against Lewis by Dr. Bacon, the chief physician of the ACS in Monrovia. Dr. Bacon added that while an American ship named *Ivanhoe* was stopping at Monrovia to drop off some trading goods belonging to Blanco, Lewis introduced him to one T. Rodriguez Buron, who was another factor of Blanco.[86] The accusation was later supported by Governor Pinney. He was said to have agreed that:

> Mr. Lewis . . . was in Blanco's employ in the slave trade in 1837; his warehouse in Monrovia was Blanco's depot for slave trade goods; that Blanco's factor did board at Lewis' house; that slavers came to Monrovia that year to get goods for the trade.[87]

Despite this accusation, Lewis was portrayed as one who frequently attended the Baptist Church, and he continually provided funds for the support of that denomination.[88] Stebbins made similar charges against such future presidents as J. J. Roberts and J. Payne and other prominent Liberians like Reverend C. Teague. Roberts was accused by contributors to the *African Repository* of going alone with Blanco's assistant, Lewis, to Sierra Leone where he bought a vessel that had been captured and condemned by the British as a slave vessel. Roberts was said to have brought the vessel to Monrovia and resold it to Blanco's factor, Buron, who in turn sent it to Gallinas where it was loaded with slaves and sent to Havana, Cuba.[89]

Stebbins' charges against the Payne family and Reverend Teague were similar to those against Lewis. Payne's house was said to be an irregular boarding place for slavers. It was also added that this role was among the main sources of income for the family. Reverend Teague was accused of allowing his "storehouse" to be used as a "slave depot" by Blanco. It was alleged that he was occasionally approached by certain prominent Liberians to provide them with one or two "slaves" for domestic work. The charge summed up that "dozens of Liberian Christians were actively and joyfully engaged in the slave trade."[90]

Even though these allegations came from only one main source, other explanations and some circumstantial evidence associated with the charges seem to give them merit. While it often editorialized that slavery had been abolished on the coast of Liberia throughout the early history of that country, the *African Repository*, which was the main journal of the ACS, occasionally admitted the contrary: that slavery existed in certain parts of coastal Liberia.[91] Although it emphasized the former in 1832-35, the journal, printed during the same period allegations that slavery existed in Cape Mount, along the St. Paul River, in Cape Palmas, Cape Montsarrado, and Little Bassa.[92]

Other observers sustained this situation. The *Liberian Herald* wrote in its 1836 edition that a British anti-slavery schooner succeeded in capturing three small Spanish slave vessels that were in the "Harbor" of Monrovia "where slaves frequently came to Wood and Water."[93] The same paper had printed that a slave vessel not far from Monrovia bought thirty slaves from the area near Monrovia.[94] Governor Pinney also admitted in 1835 that a Spanish slaver bought some slaves along the St. Paul River. It was mentioned that "the slave trade had seriously injured the colony in the last three years . . . four slave factories have been establisheed in the sight of the colony."[95] A captured letter written by a Spanish slaver at Little Bassa, presumably to a merchant in Havana, maintained that "tomorrow the schooner sails for New Sesters, to take on board a cargo of slaves. . . . I Have Been Obliged To Have One Hundred Sets of Shackles Made at Cape Mesusado. . . ."[96]

The allegation of slavery in Liberia was portrayed in slightly different form by an English naval officer named Forbes. He maintained:

> I know personally two Liberian citizens, sojourners at Cape Mount, who owned several slaves, in the general use of the term, but not its legal sense, as these were what are termed pawns, and not intended. These pawns as I have stated and believe, are as much slaves as their sable prototypes in the parent states of America, and my informants said almost all the labour in Liberia was derived form a system of domestic slavery. Of domestic slavery in Liberia there are two classes; one common to all Africa, and practiced by the aboriginal inhabitants for the most part; the other not to be complained of if not extended; of taking servants, apprentices, or pawns . . . obliging them to labour, clothing, feeding and instructing them. . . . A citizen of Liberia applied to me as a commander of one her majesty's ships, to procure for him pawns to the values of goods which he had been despoiled during the civil war at Cape Mount.[97]

Although it is labelled differently by some of the above descriptions, the labor relationship that existed between Africans and the American settlers had certain attributes that made it not much different from a master/slave relationship. The fact that the elites determined most of the relationship gives evidence to this argument. Obviously, the development of this unequal relationship was enhanced by factors that were both internal and external. As indicated earlier, before the arrival of the American settlers on the pre-Liberian coast, the society of that region had already been stratified. The new African coastal elites, who were the top layer of the new social stratification, had gained their status by exploiting both the human and natural resources of the region. This self-enriching utilization of the avialble resources had been carried out, however, in fashions similar to those later described by the various observers quoted above. Like the Liberian elites who replaced them, the pre-Liberian African coastal elites exchanged, for example, their people and tropical products such as camwood, ivory, etc., for European and later American goods.

This use of labor and the social arrangements reinforced by it were not, however, a departure from the paternalism introduced by the ACS in Liberia. Paternalism was employed in the Old South to justify religiously and racially the slaveholders' exploitation of their slaves and the social stratification called into being by that labor relationship. In other words, the labor relationship that developed in Liberia, despite the fact that it was influenced by other social forces that had developed in pre-Liberia, was similar to the one that existed between the most prominent members of the ACS and their slaves in the Old South. No wonder the ACS failed to criticize the charges brought against the elites of the Liberian colony. A critical approach to the charges would have easily exposed a basic contradiction of the prominent members of the ACS; for they too were involved with slavery, an institution they were trying, through the Liberian initiative, to abolish on the coast of West Africa.

It could, therefore, be inferred from the above explanations that the social conditions which were exploited by the Liberian elites had already been in the making when the latter arrived at what became Liberia. It would be, however, misleading to maintain that it was only these coastal social arrangements that enhanced the achievement of the

Liberian elites. As already noted, the commercial advance of the Europeans, and later the Americans, was among the principal factors that helped to make them the top layer of the newly evolving Liberian social formation. The fact that they served as middlemen between the African and foreign traders clearly showed that they did not only depend on the former traders. This is further substantiated by the fact that the Liberian elites who secretly continued to support the Atlantic slave trade did so only because there was international demand for their human goods. This was an involvement many settlers continued into the 1830s.[98] Indeed, it only ended when the Atlantic slave trade was destroyed by the new economic reality of the later nineteenth century.

This did not mean, however, that the exploitation of the Africans by the elites came to an end. Of course, the method employed was a bit different from the one that has been mentioned. Doubtless, the new evolving, modified labor relationship was directly a result of the attempt on the part of the Liberian elites to meet the new commercial requirements demanded of them by their foreign counterparts.[99] This attempt was actually intensified during the 1850s.[100] During that decade, numbers of indigenous Africans from the Liberian coast were forcibly recruited by the French to work in the West Indies. Again in 1890, some French ships were on the Liberian coast to pick up indigenous Africans to perform work on the Panama Canal and to serve in the French army, despite opposition from the Liberian government to the recruitment. But in 1892, a treaty signed between France and Liberia allowed the former to recruit Africans from Liberia for overseas duties.[101] Indeed, in 1900 several of the Liberian ruling elites signed a labor recruiting concession with a Spanish firm that was developing a cocoa plantation on the island of Fernando Po. By treaty, these elites agreed to provide most of the labor needs of the firm. It was, therefore, against this background that some 800 Kru Africans were later forcibly recruited in Liberia and shipped to the Spanish colony of Fernando Po.[102]

Although they brought wealth to certain members of the Liberian elites,[103] the foregoing labor dealings, which actually began in the early history of Liberia, did not bring meaningful economic development to the country. They obviously did little to mobilize available resources for the development of Liberia itself. In fact, by the 1870s, the national treasury of Liberia was almost without funds.[104] Doubtless, Liberian economic problems were worsened by the fact that the wealth accumulated by the Liberian elites from these labor transactions was composed of mainly non-capital goods such as western food, household materials, and clothing. Besides, the few who accumulated a large amount of capital failed to invest in such ways that would have brought a meaningful economic development to their country. They largely spent their resources on the construction of large private houses like those of their former masters of the Old South, and on more expensive American or European foodstuffs, household items, and suits of aristocratic qualities. This consuming pattern of Liberia should not be surprising for among the main objectives of the founders of the ACS was to convey to that country their social values and norms.[105]

These investing and consuming patterns were without a doubt conscious manifestations of the social distinction of Liberia's top elites. Such patterns corresponded with that country's political development which, as noted, was structured in such a way as to be dominated by the elites. It is not, therefore, surprising that the elites, perhaps consciously or unconsciously, did not encourage economic development that would have allowed capital accumulation by a relatively large number of the Liberian people, for this would have posed a serious threat to their class status.[106]

In a broader sense, however, the failure of the Liberian elites to promote progressive economic initiatives in Liberia was largely tied to the world economic system in which they participated. As implied before, their ancillary role in the promotion of the world economic system was assigned to them by the system itself. Of course, this was a logical result of a system which was not meant to bring about an egalitarian society. Indeed, as the system evolved in Europe and was promoted by the merchants of that continent throughout the world, its rewards were clearly distributed in an uneven fashion. Those who owned the means of production, such as land, factories, and capital gained more from the system than those who had nothing but their labor to sell to the former. The tremendous wealth brought to those who owned the means of production and the poverty to the many who only had their labor to offer to the system in its early development in England clearly showed that the system, even in its initial state of formation, produced wealth and poverty simultaneously.[107]

It must be pointed out, however, that as the world economic system advanced and took a more complex global form the living conditions of the working classes in European countries, such as England, the Netherlands, Belgium, France, Germany, Italy, and in the United States, were relatively improved.[108] But the minimal gains made by these classes starting from the later phase of the Industrial Revolution to the present century were won at the expense of other peoples and natural resources. The industrialization of England and the relative gains made by the working class of that country corresponded, for example, with England's world-wide exploitation of human and natural resources. England's enslavement of millions of Africans to work its American and Caribbean colonies and the wealth obtained from these functions, which indeed was used to fuel Britain's industrialization, bears testimony to this argument.[109]

In fairness to the English, it should be emphasized that the exploitation of the West African human resources was begun in the 1400s by Portugal and inherited by Spain.[110] But, as is well known, by 1713 England had inherited the monopoly of the transatlantic slave trade from Spain.[111] This coincided with England's emergence not only as supreme sea power but also as the world's supreme economic power, a role England continued to enjoy until the end of the nineteenth century.[112]

The preceding brief survey of the development of the world economy may help shed some light on why the members of the Liberian elites were unable to bring about any meaningful economic development in their country. As implied, although it was part of this economic system, Liberia had no control over it. The center, represented by Britain from the eighteenth century up to about 1900, usually determined most of the crucial functions of the system. The fact that the center usually subordinated its closer economic peripheries, as demonstrated by Britain during the period covered by this study, meant that it also determined its remote peripheries such as Liberia and other similar economically weak outposts.[113]

The economic failure of the Liberian elites could be directly associated with this argument. To better understand this, one must first consider that the economic subordination of the periphery, especially economically remote and weak peripheries such as Liberia, by the center meant that the former was rigidly locked into a specialized role that was assigned to it by the latter. This was particularly so during the period under study. Although it was a product of earlier African and European commercial interactions, the middleman role inherited by the Liberian merchant class became, for example, largely determined by the main center of the world economic system, Britain, and its immediate economic peripheries, such as continental Europe and the United States from 1822 up to the 1850s. As noted, the middleman role of the Liberian elites was radically undermined following the 1850s. The clearing of their merchant fleet from the oceans was followed by their commercial subordination by the center and immediate peripheries. They were reduced to "petty merchants" to serve the commercial firms of the center and immediate peripheries. They were easily assigned to this role by the world economic system because the ACS had not provided them with the necessary capital that would have possibly helped them to withstand external economic pressure. This together with their consuming patterns and inability to utilize fully the land and labor force of their country only enhanced their dependent outlook.

It is not, therefore, surprising that Liberia's economy was undermined by the great powers. Europe and the United States actually determined the economic relationship between Liberia and themselves. This explains why the commercial interests of the Liberian "merchant princes" were undermined as the nineteenth century drew to a close. Of course, this was largely brought about as a result of the contradictory performance of the economic system that tied Liberia to the foregoing powers. As a system of combining opposites, the world economic system even today tends to produce wealth and poverty simultaneously. While it creates employment and development for some people and countries, it, at the same time, produces the opposite for other people and countries. The presence, side-by-side, of a relatively large number of both employed and unemployed people, ghettoes and highly developed areas, extremely rich and poor even in most of the countries where the system has remarkably succeeded bears testimony to this argument. The widening economic gap that exists between the Third World and advanced countries which, in fact, have been economically tied together since the 1500s by the foregoing system gives further substantiation to the argument.[114] No wonder the national treasury of Liberia was literally empty by the 1870s. Liberia's peripheral relationship with the world economic system together with the consuming and investing patterns of the leaders of that country were the main contributors to this development.[115]

Having failed to develop their country through the exploitation of the indigenous Africans and recaptives and through their subordinate participation in the world economic system, the Liberian elites decided to attempt a modified approach. While he was visiting Britain in 1869, President Roye attempted as representative of Liberia's government to obtain a loan of about $500,000 from a British bank.[116] Although it was not immediately secured, the loan was later approved in 1871. It was approved, however, with a discount of thirty percent and an interest rate of seven percent to be paid within a period of fifteen years. The rationale behind the high discount and interest rates was that Liberia did not have valuable collateral to guarantee repayment. The result was that Liberia was to receive only $350,000 of the $500,000.[117]

Despite the fact that there was opposition to the terms of the loan in Liberia, President Roye accepted it. Of course there were reasons why President Roye acted as he did. He was a member of the declining class that needed new economic support in order to preserve its status and political leverage. This, together with the reality that Britain was the main center of the world economic system, only ensured the acceptance of the terms of the loan by Liberia as originally stipulated by the British bank.[118]

It is not surprising, therefore, that the Liberian government did not gain much from the loan. It received, for example, only about $40,000 of the $350,000 it was supposed to get. The remaining $310,000 went to private accounts of the Liberian elites and their British counterparts who had arranged the loan.[119]

Obviously, Liberia's first major loan, like most of the loans it subsequently accumulated during the period under study, did not actually contribute to its economic development; instead, it only worsened the already poor economic conditions of that country. By 1904, the national debt of Liberia was $8,000,000; and of this total, $5,000,000 had been borrowed to pay the loan of 1871 and the interest on it.[120] In fact, this pattern of borrowing to pay off previous loans and the interest on such loans became a well defined additional role assigned to Liberia by its European, and later, American creditors. This relationship, which started in 1871, continues up to the present.[121] The impact of the relationship on Liberia was obviously not advantageous. This was later described in the following way by Frederick Starr: "Debts piled upon debts, and loans calling for more loans created an alien system of financial control which seriously abridged the independence of the Republic."[122]

Just as with commerce, agriculture, and labor exploitation, borrowing from the developed world merely reinforced Liberia's subordinate role in the world economic system. Indeed, the net effect of the world economic system on the Liberian elites and the Africans they exploited was well summed up by George Brown in 1941:

> Puppets or pawns in the big game of international finance, they serve as little more than clerks or tellers of . . . Africans, retaining for themselves little more than is adequate and necessary for sustenance. Officially they have not admitted their failure to govern the country under the Western individual capitalistic system.[123]

It could be reasonably maintained, however, that the minimal material gain made by the Liberian elites from the system served them in one crucial way. It helped the elites preserve their class hegemony. Their continued social domination during the period under study gives evidence to this argument. The gain made was, however, insufficient to have brought about the emergence of a relatively large middle class in Liberia. As noted before, contributing to the failure of the elites to do so were their consuming and investing patterns. The elites' social domination which was largely economically based and determined, was not only manifested by their lifestyle, but it was also illustrated by their political supremacy that lasted throughout the period under consideration. But this domination, was irregularly challenged, sometimes verbally and at other times physically, by the people who were not accommodated by the system. The first reaction took place in 1823 when Governor Ashmun was forced out of the Liberian colony by the settlers. Similar events occurred in 1871 when President Roye was overthrown and later mysteriously killed by his mulatto opponents and again in 1980 when the administration of President Tolbert was violently vanquished.

These social disruptions, coupled with the fact that Liberia remains an underdeveloped country, clearly illustrate the fact that the subordinate participation of the Liberian elites in the world economic system benefited Liberia only narrowly. The failure of the Liberian elites to gain from the system was not, however, completely of their own making, as some scholars have tried to suggest.[124] In the first place, their participation was not deliberate. With no doubt the early groups of settlers sent to Liberia had little choice but to look up to the ACS for leadership and material support. They could not have survived without such assistance. This was more so since the African slave traders and their counterparts from the western world were hostile to the colony. They viewed it as a threat to their trade in human beings. This, together with the social backgrounds of the settlers and the ACS which administered them, ensured the settlers' dependent outlook. The paternalistic relationship that emerged between the ACS and the settlers took economic form as Liberia grew. This was further reinforced when European and American traders began to penetrate Liberia.

At this juncture, it can be maintained that Liberia's dependent economic formation was a manifestation of the various social forces at work in that country. Its development was ensured by the fact that there was no social force, either internal or external, to challenge it seriously. This statement could well be applied to the social system introduced in Liberia by the ACS. Liberia's paternalistic social arrangements helped to facilitate its social stratification and dependent relationship with the ACS. This development corresponded with the ancillary role the world economic system assigned to Liberia. In other words, the world economic system and the social values introduced by the ACS had a lot in common. No wonder they tended to accommodate each other though the process was not always concordant.

It must be pointed out, however, that as Liberia advanced, its economic formation became increasingly determined by the world economic system. The latter's success at assigning Liberia to specific roles such as exporter of raw materials and importer of industrial goods bears testimony to this argument. Liberia could not possibly have achieved a meaningful economic development through these roles. The net gain made from such economic roles was not immense. Besides, the gain was composed of mostly consumer goods.

Still there is the question: why then did Liberia fail to disengage itself from the system? The answer is that Liberia could not possibly have carried out this attempt easily. To understand this, one must consider first what has been illustrated throughout this chapter: that from its beginning in 1822, Liberia inherited an historical process that ensured its continued engagement with the world economic system. The commercial orientation of the pre-Liberian coast to meet the requirements of the world economic system and the reinforcement of this development by the ACS through its paternalistic arrangements gives evidence of this.

These trends were further reinforced by the fact that although it was not gaining much from the system in general, Liberian elites were benefiting tremendously. The social status and the continued class supremacy of the members of this group during the period under study bear testimony to this. It is not, surprising, therefore, that they did not make any serious attempt to change or modify their involvement with the system. Nevertheless, taking into consideration its overall impact on Liberia, it can be concluded that such an involvement with the world economic system, inevitably the result of a heritage of dependency started by the ACS, not only failed to bring economic development to Liberia, but it also continued to make that country vulnerable to social violence.

NOTES

Chapter V

[1]See Chapter IV for this explanation.

[2]It was incapable of expanding on its own. For this definition, See Cardoso and Faletto, *Dependency and Development in Latin America*, pp. xx-xvi.

[3]*African Repository*, I, p. 219.

[4]"Latest from Liberia, 1827-1828," *The African Observer*, Vol. 1-2, p. 286.

[5]*African Repository*, I, p. 219.

[6]Ashmun to the ACS (July, 1823) in Gurley's *Life of Jehudi Ashmun*, Appendix, pp., 50-52.

[7]*Ibid.*, pp. 57-59.

[8]*Ibid.*, p. 60.

[9]West, *Back to Africa*, p. 133.

[10]Gurley, *Life of Jehudi Ashmun*, Appendix, p. 64.

[11]*Ibid.*, p. 64.

[12]West, *Back to Africa*, pp. 126-27.

[13]For the effects of the Atlantic slave trade on the pre-Liberian coast, see Chapter II.

[14]*The ACS Papers*, Vol. (1826), p. 81.

[16]James L. Sibley, *Liberia* (New York, 1928), pp. 113-152.

[17]Brown, *The Economic History of Liberia*, p. 118.

[18]*Ibid.*

[19]Edmund Ruffin, *American Colonization Unveiled*, pp. 20-21.

[20]See these works for specific explanations for this argument: L. S. Stavrianos, *Global Rift: The Third World Comes of Age* (New York, 1981), pp. 116-117, 202-203; Michael Beaud, *A History of Capitalism, 1500-1980* (New York, 1983), p. 44; Amin, *Imperialism and Unequal Development*, pp., 117-136; ______, *Accumulation on a World Scale* (New York, 1974), p. 199; ______, *Unequal Development* (New York, 1976), p. 226; Rodney, *A History of the Upper Guinea*, pp. 152-221, 240-270; Fyfe, "The Dynamics of African Dispersal: The Transatlantic Slave Trade," pp. 64-74; and Mandel, *Late Capitalism*, pp. 342-376.

[21]*Ibid.*

[22]The consuming pattern of the Liberian ruling elites was not much different from their former masters in the Old South. For this argument, see Starobin, *Industrial Slavery*, Chapter 6; Pennsylvania Anti-Slavery Society, *Address to the Coloured People of the State of Pennsylvania* (Philadelphia, 1837), p. 6; Randall M. Miller, ed., *Dear Master: Letters of Slave Families* (Ithaca, 1978), pp. 47-50; and Stebbins, *Facts and Opinions*, pp. 184-85.

[23]Stebbins, *Facts and Opinions*, pp. 169-172.

[24]According to some accounts, the first palm kernels to be exported to Europe from West Africa were arranged by a Liberian. See Sir Harry Johnston, *Liberia*, Vol. 2 (New York, 1906), p. 403.

[25]*The American Colonization Society Bulletin in Liberia* (Washington, 1853), pp. 1-2.

[26]Commonwealth Legislative Minutes, 1837-1847.

[27]*African Repository*, XXVIII (1851), p. 100.

[28]Fyfe, *A History of Sierra Leone*, pp. 14-19.

[29]Huberich, *The Political and Legislative History*, Vol. I, p. 772-784.

[30]*Ibid.*, pp. 772-775; and Yancy, *Historical Light of Liberia*, p. 54.

[31]Minutes of the Senate, 1849-1892, Liberian National Archives (Monrovia).

[32]Schick, *Behold the Promised Land*, p. 104.

[33]*Ibid.*

[34]Dwight N. Syfert, "The Liberian Coasting Trade, 1822-1900," *Journal of African History*, Vol. XVIII (1977), p. 229.

[35]For details of this argument see Johnston's *Liberia*, pp. 242-250, and Brown, *The Economic History of Liberia*, pp. 160-162.

[36]Republic of Liberia, Treaties and Conventions Concluded Between Liberia and Foreign Powers, 1847-1907, Liberian National Archives (Monrovia).

[37]*Ibid.*

[38]*Ibid.*

[39]*Ibid.*

[40]See note 36.

[41]Republic of Liberia, Treaties and Conventions.

[42]Gabriel L. Dannis, Brief Outline of Liberia-German Relations. Liberian National Archives (Monrovia).

[43]Syfert, "The Liberian Coasting Trade, 1822-1900." p. 229.

[44]*Ibid.*, p. 223.

[45]*African Repository*, XLIX (1873), p. 214; *New Era*, March 20, 1873.

[46]*The Observer*, December 25, 1879.

[47]Syfert, "The Liberian Coasting Trade, 1822-1900," p. 223.

[48]Karnga, *The History of Liberia*, p. 41.

[49]*Ibid.*, pp. 41-42.

[50]Shick, *Behold the Promised Land*, p. 112.

[51]*Ibid.*

[52]*Ibid.*, p. 113.

[53]Franklin W. Knight, *Slave Society in Cuba in the Nineteenth Century* (Madison, 1970), p. 44.

[54]Brown, *The Economic History of Liberia*, pp. 125, 134, and 140.

[55]Shick, *Behold the Promised Land*, p. 116.

[56]McPherson, *A History of Liberia*, p. 49.

[57]Shick, *Behold The Promised Land*, p. 116; Webster and Boahan, *The Revolutionary Years*, p. 113.

[58]Webster and Boahen, *The Revolutionary Years*, p. 133.

[59] *The American Colonization Society Bulletin in Liberia* (Washington, 1895), p. 8.

[60] Allen McPhee, *The Economic Revolution of British West Africa* (London, 1926), p. 30.

[61] Woodruff D. Smith, *The German Colonial Empire* (Chapel Hill, 1978), pp. 119-125.

[62] Johnston, *Liberia*, p. 398; E. A. Forbes, *The Land of the White Helmet Lights and Shadows Across Africa* (New York, n.d.), p. 230.

[63] H. Wauwerman, *Liberia* (Brussels, 1885), p. 230.

[64] Brown, *The Economic History of Liberia*, p. 159.

[65] *Ibid.*, p. 160; Wauwerman, *Liberia*, p. 250.

[66] Brown, *The Economic History of Liberia*, p. 160.

[67] *Ibid.*, p. 143.

[68] *Ibid.*, p. 160.

[69] For this argument, see note 2 and Bade onimode, *Imperialism and Underdevelopment in Nigeria* (London, 1982), pp. 42-67.

[70] *Ibid.* See also note 20 for this argument.

[71] Cardoso and Faletto, *Dependency and Development*, pp. vii-xxv.

[72] Brown, *The Economic History of Liberia*, pp. 143-160.

[73] Wauwerman, *Liberia*, p. 205.

[74] The British sent a gunboat to Monrovia to make sure that the treaty was accepted by Liberia. For this explanation, see R. L. F. Maugham, *Republic of Liberia* (London, 1921), p. 97.

[75]Buell, *Native Problem in Africa*, Vol. II, p. 785.

[76]*Ibid.*, p. 125.

[77]See note 15.

[78]Shick, in his *Behold the Promised Land* implied that settlers' plantations were worked mostly by the recaptives. This explanation is, however, based on one example. Shick, *Behold the Promised Land*, p. 113. On the other hand, Brown in his *Economic History of Liberia*, maintained that settlers' plantations were entirely worked by indigenous Africans. See Brown, *The Economic History of Liberia*, pp. 116-117 for this argument.

[79]Maugham, *The Republic of Liberia*, p. 82.

[80]Stebbins, *Facts and Opinions*, pp. 175-176.

[81]Elder S. S. Ball was a black American Baptist clergyman who was sent to Liberia by his church in 1848 to investigate the conditions of that country. His observations of Liberia was later published as a pamphlet entitled: *Liberia: The Conditions and Prospects of the Republic* (Alton, 1848). For details of his accounts of Liberia, see Stebbins, *Facts and Opinions*, pp. 184- 188.

[82]Matilda R. Lomax, from Monrovia, November 23, 1849 to General J. H. C. Shields Wilson, deposit, Cocke Papers, cited in Miller, ed., *Dear Master:*, pp. 103-04. Also cited in Bell I. Wiley, ed., *Slave No More Letters from Liberia 1833-1869* (Lexington, 1980), pp. 69-70.

[83]*The African Repository*, (1849), p. 80; Stebbins, *Facts and Opinions*, p. 177.

[84]Stebbins, *Facts and Opinions*, pp. 41-42.

[85]Quoted in Karnga, *History of Liberia*, pp. 41-42.

[86]Stebbins, *Facts and Opinions*, p. 162.

[87]Quoted in *Ibid.*

[88]*Ibid.*

[89]*Ibid.*

[90]*Ibid.*

[91]*Ibid.*, pp. 162-163.

[92]*African Repository*, XX (1836), pp. 120-123.

[93]Cited in *Ibid.*

[94]*Liberian Herald* (1836)

[95]*African Repository*, XIX (1837), p. 110.

[96]This letter was published by the British Parliament on September 28, 1838. For the details of its publication, see Stebbins, *Facts and Opinions*, p. 160.

[97]Quoted in *Ibid.*, pp. 164-165.

[98]For a detailed explanation of this, see *Ibid.*, especially pp. 155-167.

[99]For details see: Brown, *The Economic History of Liberia*, pp. 158-163; Johnston, *Liberia*, pp. 241-249; Buell, *Native Problem in Africa*, Vol. II, p. 784; W. E. B. DuBois, "Liberia and Rubber," *New Republic* (November, 1925), pp. 326-329.

[100]Brown, *The Economic History of Liberia*, p. 147.

[101]Buell, *The Native Problem in Africa*, Vol. II, p. 777.

[102]For details of this example, see these works: Sundiata, *Black Scandal*, especially Chapters 1, 2, and 6; ______, "Creolization on the Fernando Po: The Nature of Society," in Kilson and Rotberg, eds., *The African Diaspora*, pp. 391-413; and Brown, *The Economic History of Liberia*, pp. 148-152.

[103]Liberian officials such as President Charles D. B. King, Vice President Allen N. Yancy, Postmaster General Samuel Ross, and District Commissioner P. C. Lenandine doubtless benefited materially from the labor contract that existed between Liberia and Fernando Po. For details of this see note 102 above, especially Brown, *The Economic History of Liberia*, pp. 150-152.

[104]*Ibid.*, pp. 142-145.

[105]*Ibid.*, pp. 108, 117, 137-138; Johnston, *Liberia*, pp. 360-369; and Stebbins, *Facts and Opinions*, pp. 185-186.

[106]Stebbins, *Facts and Opinions*, pp. 185-187.

[107]For this line of argument, see the following works: Cardoso and Faletto, *Dependency and Development*, pp. xxiii-xxiv; Onimode, *Imperialism and Underdevelopment in Nigeria*, pp. 3-9; Beaud, *A History of Capitalism*, pp. 17-42.

[108]Beaud, *A History of Capitalism*, pp. 17-74; Paul N. Sweezy, *Theory of Capitalist Development: Principles of Marxian Political Economy* (New York, 1942), pp. 290-291.

[109]Fyfe, "The Dynamics of the African Dispersal," pp. 64-66; Beaud, *A History of Capitalism*, pp. 27-29; Donald C. Gordon, *The Movement of Power: Britain's Imperial Epoch* (Englewood Cliffs, 1970), pp. 4-18.

[110]For this argument, see Boxer, *Four Centuries of Portuguese Expansion*, especially pp. 23-25. For the inheritance of the role by Spain, see *Ibid.*, pp. 9-13; Mannix and Cowley, *Black Cargoes*, pp. 1-3.

[111]Parry, *The Establishment of European Hegemony*, pp. 158-159; Dunn, *Sugar and Slaves*, pp. 146-148; Carrington, *The British Overseas*, pp. 62-65.

[112]Beaud, *A History of Capitalism*, pp. 122-125; Harry Magdoff and Paul M. Sweezy, *The End of Prosperity: The American Economy in the 1970s* (New York, 1977), pp. 55-63; Sidney Lens, *The Forging of the American Empire: A History of American Imperialism From the Revolution to Vietnam* (New York, 1974), pp. 275-291, 312, 331-332, 338-343, 349-365. The United States was to inherit this role from Britain. By the first quarter of the twentieth century, it

was increasingly emerging not only as a world military power but also as a supreme economic power. The very fact that the home base of the world economic system shifted from England to the United States meant that the latter could determine that system almost at will. It is not therefore surprising that the American dollar became the standard of the world economic system.

[113]For details of this argument, see note 20.

[114]*Ibid.*

[115]Brown, *The Economic History of Liberia*, pp. 142-145; Johnston, *Liberia*, p. 402; and Nnamdi Azikiwe, *Liberia in World Politics* (London, 1934), p. 119.

[116]Starr, *Liberia: Description, History, and Problem*, p. 119.

[117]Brown, *The Economic History of Liberia*, p. 143.

[118]During this period, the United States was too busy promoting its economic interest in its western region, Latin America, and in other places to have possibly committed itself seriously to the burning problems of Liberia.

[119]Wauwerman, *Liberia*, p. 159.

[120]Buell, *Native Problem in Africa*, Vol. II, pp. 443-444.

[121]Currently, Liberia owes the industrialized world, especially the United States more than $700,000,000.

[122]Starr, *Liberia: Description, History, and Problem*, p. 205.

[123]Brown, *The Economic History of Liberia*, p. 250.

[124]Works that have treated Liberia's economic failure in isolation include: M. B. Akpan, "Black Imperialism: Americo-Liberian Rule Over the African Peoples of Liberia, 1822-1964," *Canadian Journal of African Studies*, Vol. VII (1973); Lowenkopf, Politics in Liberia: The Conservative Road to Developmentnd George Dalton, "History and Economic Development in Liberia," *Journal of Economic History*, Vol. XXV (1965).

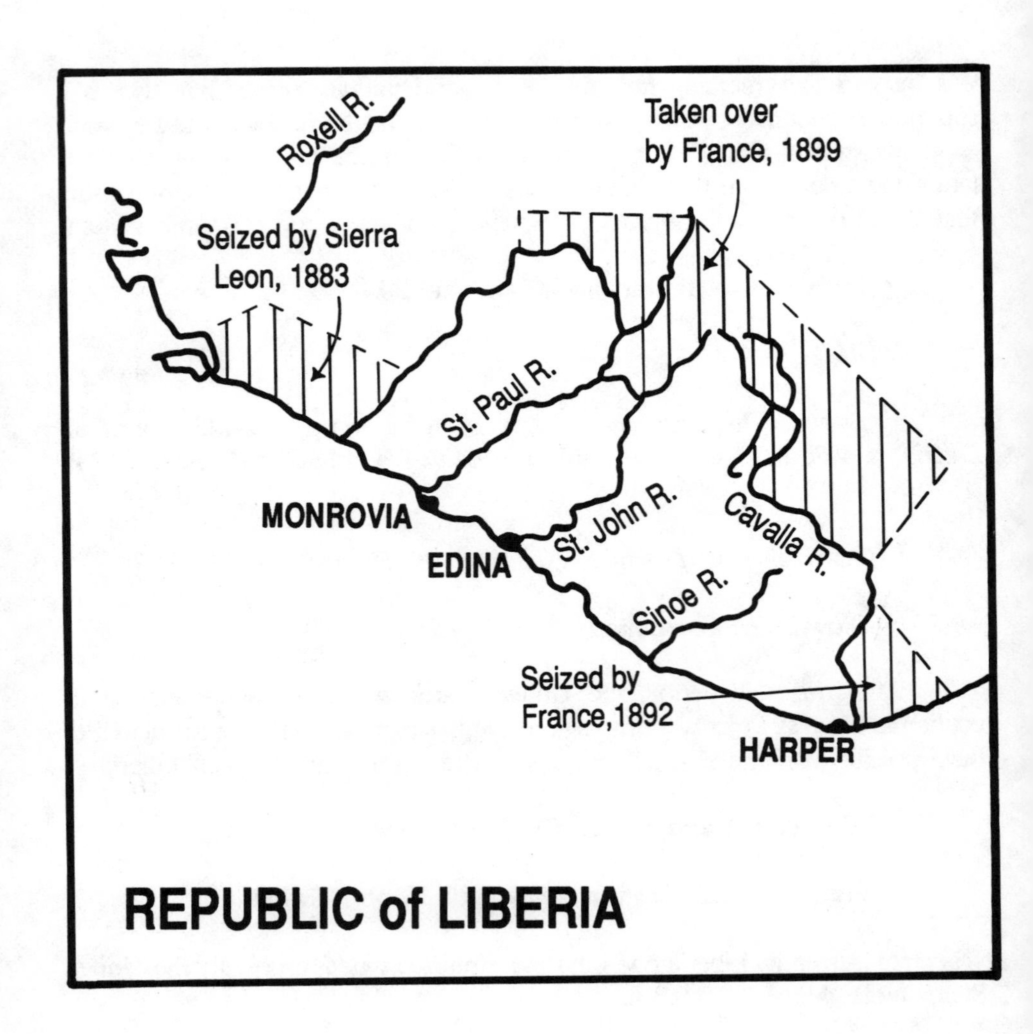
Roxell R.
Taken over
by France, 1899
Seized by Sierra
Leon, 1883
St. Paul R.
MONROVIA
St. John R.
Cavalla R.
EDINA
Sinoe R.
Seized by
France,1892
HARPER
REPUBLIC of LIBERIA

CHAPTER VI

RELIGION AND SOCIAL CHANGE

PRODUCED BY THE AMERICAN COLONIZATION SOCIETY

Although other social arrangements, such as family ties, kinship, and group solidarity helped to give shape to its peculiar characteristics, Liberia's prescribed social behavior was largely influenced by either the various religious values inherent in the ACS or the ones approved by that organization. Even the settlers' family characteristics and structural forms were mostly governed by the ACS's values.[1] Indeed, the religious ethos and norms of the ACS served as main determinants of social behavior in Liberia. These values not only influenced personal behavior, but also reinforced the political culture of paternalism and the way in which the American colonists and their descendants came to view what they termed "civilization."

Many observers noted the tremendous impact of American religious values on nineteenth century Liberia. One of the most perceptive was Sir Harry Johnston, the British Africanist and later colonial administrator, who was an occasional visitor to the country in the 1880s. Sir Harry noted the all-encompassing impact of religion in his descriptive book on Liberia.

> With a few rare exceptions, the Americo-Liberian community suffers from religiosity. . . . They are Episcopalians . . . Methodists, Baptists, Presbyterians, Lutherans, Zionists, and so forth. . . . They exhibit the Puritanism of New England in the eighteenth century almost unabated. Their average morality is probably no higher than that of the European nations or even of the Negroes indigenous to Liberia. But so far as outward behavior, laws, and language go, they are prudish to a truly

> American extent. Sparsity of clothing on the part of the natives is treated in some settlements as an offence. . . . The Americo-Liberian still worships cloths as an outward and visible manifestation of Christianity and the best civilization; that is to say, the European cloths of the nineteenth century. . . . No self-respecting Liberian would be seen on . . . a Sunday . . . even under a broiling sun . . . except in an immaculate black silk topper and a long black frock coat. Their women of course follow the fashion of Europe. . . .[2]

This quotation is not an inaccurate description of Liberia's social character, especially if it is applied to the period under consideration. The first groups of immigrants sent to what became Liberia were deeply religious. Indeed among the leaders of the immigrants were Reverend Waring, a Baptist minister, and Reverend Coker, a Methodist preacher. They were authorized by the ACS to provide for the spiritual needs of the anticipated settlement. It is not, therefore, surprising that the Baptist Church became the first and most influential church in Liberia.[3] It was followed by the Episcopal Church which began religious activities in Liberia in 1830. By the later 1830s, the Methodist Episcopal and the Presbyterian Churches had begun missionary activities in Liberia. And by the 1880s, the African Methodist Episcopal Church, which was exclusively for Black Americans, and the Lutheran Church had established themselves in Liberia.[4]

The religious and secular impacts of these denominations on Liberia were indeed tremendous. Between 1822 and 1885, these denominations established churches in almost every settlement in Liberia. Most of the activities of the Baptist Church were limited to the Monrovia and Bassa settlements. The Episcopal Church was active in every settlement, even in the Maryland settlement which did not become part of Liberia until 1857. In fact, every settlement had churches or schools that were in one way or another affiliated with the denomination. Before the 1880s, it had built beautiful, large churches in Cape Mount and Cape Palmas. Its establishment included a bishop, 18 ministers, 69 well committed catechumen, "38 day schools, 18 boarding schools, and 31 Sunday schools." About 3,000 students were enrolled in its schools.[5]

The Methodist Episcopal Church had 2,700 followers, 48 clergymen, 40 nonprofessional teachers, "59 Sunday schools," and 2,709 students in its schools.[6] The Presbyterian Church, which began missionary performances in the same year the Methodists arrived in that country, was mainly confined to Monrovia and the Upriver settlers. The African Methodist Episcopal Church became active in Monteserrado, Sino, and Bassa Counties. The Lutheran Church carried on most of its missionary and educational activities in the Upriver region. It succeeded in establishing schools, churches, and clinics in such Upriver settlements as Whiteplains, Arthington, and Mount Coffee.[7]

The effects of the roles of the various Christian denominations on Liberia cannot be underestimated, especially if one is to understand the social characteristics of the country. As noted, the activities of these churches in Liberia were not only limited to the promotion of the gospel, they also included preparation for the secular world. The first western educational instutions were, for example, established by these denominations. In one crucial way, these American-based churches were indeed conveying to Liberia America's institutional values. These values included American social ethics and the concept of a "civilized" person. It is not surprising that almost uniquely American educational systems as "the common schools of New England, the high schools and academies of New York and lyceums and lectures of Pennsylvania" were introduced in Liberia by these denominations.[8]

American Protestant spiritual and secular views largely comprised this educational system. They were designed to make individual characters conform to the approved social norms. One Jabez A. Burton, who headed the Methodist Seminary in Liberia, spelled out the educational objective when he stipulated in 1838 that the aim of his school was "to elevate the character, suppress every wrong motive, to strengthen every good principle, and to prepare the subject . . . for ever. . . ." The teachers who taught at his school were encouraged to emphasize" . . . love of order, diligence, and morality." He also added that the role of his school was " . . . one of which children can be taught--young persons receive instructions--and all be aided in their endeavors the better to serve God and their country."[9] Indeed, the Methodist Church summarized its educational aims in Liberia in this way in 1850:

> The great end aimed at will be to give these youth a plain education, to lead them to adopt the modes and habits of civilized life, to train them, and rear them up as Christians, and bring them to adopt such habits of industry and economy, as that, when no longer supported by the mission, they may be found good citizens, well able to take care of themselves.[10]

The Methodist Church and other Christian churches in Liberia established educational institutions in the country to carry out the realization of such aims. Both technical and academic subjects were emphasized in these schools. The former emphasized agricultural skills, and the latter theology and traditional liberal disciplines.[11]

Taken as a whole, the effect of religious education on Liberia was greater than those of secular teachings. There were several reasons for this. First and most important, the various denominations in Liberia tended to give more consideration to the former than the latter. Of course, this was in line with their main aim, which was to spread the gospel in Liberia. Enhancing this development was the fact that the Liberian secular leaders held that the inception of Liberia was part of God's divine plan. As discussed before, this view was conveyed to Liberia by the ACS, and later inherited and internalized by the people of that country.

Indeed the internalization and articulation of the various religious views by the immigrant Liberians were without doubt systematically reinforced by the churches involved and the ACS. Those immigrants who closely indentified with and effectively expressed the various religious views were, for example, made the leaders of their people. This statement could well be applied to nearly all prominent Liberian leaders who served during the period under consideration.[12] No wonder their secular views were not distinguishable from their non-secular views.

This was eloquently demonstrated during colonial Liberia and greatly emphasized in independent Liberia. All Liberia's governors from Ayres to Roberts led Liberia almost as if the territory were a religious colony. They all appealed to the settlers to be religious and to conform to the values introduced by the various denominations in Liberia. Indeed, as early as 1827, Governor Ashmun had recommended to the ACS that the settlers should be Christianized in the following ways:

> . . . it be an influence from without, motives applied and forces upon them by the benevolent care and labor of others, which is to arouse and engage them in the great and principle work of life--the cultivation of rational and immortal natures. The precepts and doctrines of Jesus Christ, from Alpha to Omega, must be inculcated with Apostological earnestness and perseverance, and I may add, pedagogical precision, too, before they can become Christians. . . .[13]

Ashmun was to add that through God's grace, an achievement " . . . so agreeable to the great ends of his moral government . . ." would be made in Liberia. He went on to conclude that the foundation of the settlers' government must be "holiness."[14]

As suggested, the foregoing emphasis was not only heard during the colonial era, but it was also emphasized after independence. In his inaugural address, Liberia's first President, Roberts, declared, for example, that:

> The Gospel, fellow citizens is yet to be preached to vast numbers inhabiting this dark continent, and I have the highest reason to believe, that was one of the great objects of the Almighty in establishing colonies, that they might be the means of introducing civilization and religion among the barbarous nations of this country; and to what work more noble could our powers be applied than that of bringing up from darkness, debasement, and misery, our fellow men, and shedding abroad over them the light of science and Christianity.[15]

President Roberts' successor, Benson, was to declare that Liberia had been blessed by God providing leaders who were suitable for the period during which they were appointed to conduct the affairs of that country. Like all Liberian presidents, Benson maintained that the inception and destiny of Liberia were predetermined by God.[16] With this view, he argued that Liberia's guiding values were to be governed by those of God. And these values were to be internalized and articulated by all Liberians. To make his call more appealing to his audience, Benson gave the illusion " . . . that there is no people . . . on earth of equal number, charged with a more important mission by Providence, and consequently upon whom devolve more weighty political and religious obligations . . . than the people of Liberia."[17]

Even Presidents Warner and Roye, who tended to treat secular issues in secular contexts, were influenced by the foregoing religious impulse. In his first inaugural address, President Warner declared that:

> I believe that that Great Being who planted us on these shores, and who has so kindly protected us, will continue to protect us if we put our trust in Him. He will bear down and remove every hindrance to our progress. The mighty wheels of His Providence are in operation, and those who will not move along with them will be ground to powder. If the cutting off of a right hand or the plucking out of a right eye be necessary to the ultimate success of Liberia in all her various interests, I believe that in the administration of Providence we shall lose that right hand and be deprived of that right eye.[18]

In his last inaugural address, President Warner maintained that God was the main determinant of Liberia, which, according to him, was in the interest of that country.[19]

President Roye, who was to a degree like Warner, also emphasized religious aspects, though in a lesser way. Like his predecessors and nearly all those who served after him, President Roye believed that God had allowed the "cruel" enslavement of those who later immigrated to Liberia as a means of preparing them to promote western civilization and Christianity in that country. In his first and last inaugural address, President Roye declared:

> Fellow citizens, I regard the Liberian nation as sacred. God has planted us here; and through all the vicissitudes of our existence, his hand has been plainly, visibly directing our

affairs. . . . He has supplied our deficiencies and enlightened our ignorances. . . .[20]

Indeed, as Liberia moved toward the twentieth century, religious sentiment was increasingly.becoming very dogmatic. This development, no doubt, was influenced by the fact that religion could easily be used to explain complex social issues. Liberian leaders were oftentimes inclined to attribute the economic or political failure of their country to Providence. Such a shifting of responsibility was enhanced by the acceptance of the idea that the Liberian entity was God's creation. And, of course, since this was the generally held view, it was further accepted that Liberia's social developments, whether success or failure, might have been predetermined by God.

Despite the fact that this was not in any way a critical approach to the various problems that confronted Liberia, it served the Liberian leaders in one crucial way. It enabled them to veil their political and other mistakes. No wonder Christian thoughts and values were encouraged, or in some cases, made compulsory, in Liberia. Sunday, fo example, was lawfully set aside as a day of worship and rest, and newspapers provided large spaces for pointless explanations of the Old and New Testaments.[21]

Because the top layer of Liberian society emphasized these emerging values, those in the middle and bottom of that social order were influenced to become more receptive to them. Two factors ensured this receptive response to this religious emphasis. As noted earlier, one of the ways of climbing Liberia's social ladder was indeed the serious acceptance and eloquent articulation of those values put forward by the various leaders of that country. Besides, the social backgrounds of those who immigrated from the New World to Liberia were the same as the ones that were being emphasized in the latter. It is not surprising, therefore, that these values were internalized and then outwardly expressed by the masses of the immigrant Liberians.

Indeed, letters written by some of the immigrants to their relatives, friends, or former masters in America clearly show their spiritual feelings.[22] Lomax, an immigrant, emphasized in a letter written to her former master, John H. Cocke, that she was training her children " . . .

in the fear of the Lord."[23] She went on to add that although she was not sure she would again see him on this earth, she was confident that they would meet each other in heaven.[24] A Monrovian settler, Robert L. Sterdivant, explained in his letter to one Sally C. Brent that the latter should tell her slaves that he was in " . . . the Land of the Living . . . God," and he and his children were being cared for by Providence.[25] One ordinary settler reemphasized the spiritual sentiment of Liberia when he said that:

> . . . there are two principal gentlemen strictly and purely Liberian[s] which are S. A. Benson and J. J. Roberts. The light that led them this far was light from heaven. I believe that Liberia will yet stand with the other parts of the Civilized World. O praise the Lord all ye nations! Praise Him all ye people for His merciful kindness is Great toward us and the truth of the Lord endureth for ever! [P]raise the Lord![26]

One other settler, Washington W. McDonogh, emphasized that he was fortunate that he had not been enslaved by a non-Christian country. The effects of his religious belief and the social culture of paternalism on him were demonstrated when he maintained that " . . . praise His holy name, that my former master was not a weakened person, that he treated me as a son 'instead' of as a slave." He concluded by charging that " . . . an honest man is said to be the noblest work of his Creator. Had I· been permitted to run about, as many of my age were, I should have been today as ignorant as they are; but, thanks be to my Creator, I was not."[27]

This emphasis was further repeated by another Liberian immigrant in a letter written to his former master, thus:

> . . . we thank God day and night that we cast our lot under so kind a master as you, sir, who helped us with our riches to get here, to this free and blessed land of our fathers, where the colored man can be happy, if he will . . . love and walk with God. Our hearts overflow, sir, when we think of you and all you have done for us poor black people. But the great God whom you serve, who you taught us to serve,

> has blessed you, wonderfully blessed you, and will continue to bless you, through many days yet to come here on earth, and will translate you when your days are ended, we trust into His heavenly kingdom. All of which, we your poor black friends here in Africa, pray for day and night.[28]

In fact, most of the letters written by the immigrants to their relatives or former masters in America during the period under study reflected their deep religious motivation.[29] Not only were they religious, but their outward social behavior was heavily influenced by their religious sentiment. The term "civilized" was used in Liberia, for example, to describe people who were Christians. Of course, this meant that they wore western clothes and spoke English. The beginning of the usage could be traced back to the inception of Liberia in 1822.[30] Indeed, the term was still used in Liberia in this sense up until the 1960s.[31]

The fact that all the black Americans who immigrated to Liberia were to a degree westernized, automatically qualified them to be described as "civilized" people. The recaptives and indigenous Africans who became acculturated into these religious and social values were also accepted, though reluctantly, as "civilized" Liberians.[32] In other words, while the "door" for such a social accommodation was opened, it was not opened wide enough, especially to the indigenous Africans. From 1822 until the 1960s, only a small number of the indigenous Africans were, for example, considered as fully "civilized."[33]

It must be pointed out that the few who were accommodated were consistently reminded to conceal their traditional social values and increasingly manifest their acquired ones. This explained why the indigenous Africans who became "civilized" were nothing but imitators of the immigrant Liberians. They took, for instance, western or Christian names, spoke English, dressed and outwardly behaved like the settler Liberians. As the former, the latter tended to describe nearly every indigenous African social institution as "uncivilized," or unchristian. It became very difficult to distinguish socially the two groups. This applied especially to the few indigenous "civilized" Liberians who succeeded in becoming members of the upper layers of the Liberian social structure.[34]

But despite the fact that this process brought social distinction to the settler and a few of the indigenous Liberians, it had a number of serious shortcomings. As noted before, its tremendous emphasis on the Christian religion and social values created conditions whereby the settlers and the few "civilized" indigenous Liberians began to accept that their main guiding principles should be those inherent in the religious doctrine. Not only were they influenced by the doctrine, but they also manipulated it in ways to promote their social uniqueness and to achieve their secular objectives. But in the attempt of accomplishing this, two main social concepts were reinforced that obviously were not in the interests of the development of Liberia as a whole.

The acceptance of the idea that Liberia was God's creation and its success or failure was indeed predetermined by Providence, first of all, created an atmosphere whereby the failures or blunders of the Liberian rulers were easily attributed to God. While this helped to secure the leverage and the leadership of the individuals in question, it made Liberia's elites unable to treat critically the various social problems of that country. No wonder the rice riot which occurred in Liberia in 1979 was described by Liberian authorities as an "act of evil spirits."[35]

Relating to the preceding argument is that this trend, secondly, distorted very painfully what a civilized society meant. Instead of it being viewed as a society that has achieved a relatively higher level of cultural and technological development in an orderly manner,[36] the term was defined in Liberia as those who became Christians, spoke English, and dressed or behaved like westerners.

But such a gross distortion was to have serious ill effects on Liberia. As implied before, it contributed to the feeble economic and political developments that were already shaping Liberia in a way whereby the cultural and technological underdevelopment of the country was reinforced. This was heightened by the fact that the term *civilized*, as used in the Liberian context, did not mean cultural or technological build up. No wonder Liberia was to be described later in the twentieth century as an "intellectual desert."[37]

Taking such arguments into consideration, it is obvious that these religious norms, which were conveyed to Liberia first and many times over by the ACS, had an enormous impact on education, social behavior, and the way the Liberian elites viewed society. This represented a success for the "civilizing mission" of the ACS, but those same religious values also had an extremely negative impact on Liberia. They were among the obstacles to the overall meaningful development of that country. In this sense, the "civilizing mission," which was among the objectives the ACS had hoped to accomplish on the West African coast, was ironically undermined by that movement.

NOTES

Chapter VI

[1]With no doubt, the settlers' family structures, form, kinship, solidarity to each other, and their African physical and social environments affected their social manifestations in Liberia. Shick has treated this aspect of Liberian society in his *Behold the Promised Land*. See especially his Chapters Three, Four and Five. Nevertheless, the various religious values embedded in the ACS and the ones approved by that movement were the main determinants of Liberia's outward social behavior.

[2]Johnston, *Liberia*, pp. 353-354.

[3]*Ibid.*, p. 376.

[4]*Ibid.*, pp. 375-376.

[5]*Ibid.*, p. 374.

[6]*Ibid.*, pp. 374-376. Reverend Scott was under the control of Bishop J. C. Hartzell who supervised nearly all American missionary works between the coastal area of Liberia and Angola. His leadership was later extended to include Rhodesia and Mozambique. He was mainly stationed in the United States.

[7]Johnston, *Liberia*, p. 376.

[8]Henry J. Drewal, "Methodist Education in Liberia, 1833-1856," in Vincent M. Battle and Charles H. Lyons, eds., *Essays in the History of African Education* (New York, 1970), p. 33.

[9]Cited in *Ibid.*, p. 47. See also the *Africa's Luminary* (1837), p. 27.

[10]Cited in Drewal, "Methodist Education in Liberia, 1833-1856," pp. 33-34.

[11]Johnston, *Liberia*, p. 389.

[12]For details of this argument, see Chapters IV and V.

[13]Ashmun to the ACS, May 20, 1827 in Gurley's, *Life of Ashmun*, Appendix, p. 36.

[14]*Ibid.*, p. 38.

[15]*African Repository*, XXIV (1848), p. 125.

[16]*Ibid.*, XXXII (1856), pp. 200, 203.

[17]*Ibid.*, XXXVIII (1862), p. 98.

[18]*Ibid.*, XL (1864), p. 108.

[19]Presidential Address, (Monrovia, 1866).

[20]*African Repository*, XLVI (1870), p. 106.

[21]Johnstone, *Liberia*. p. 358.

[22]It must be pointed out, however, that some of these letters were written in such ways as to get material aids from the former masters of those who wrote.

[23]Matilda Lomax, from Monrovia, September 26, 1853, to John H. Cocke, deposit Cocke Papers, quoted in Wiley, ed., *Slave No More*, p. 78.

[24]*Ibid.*

[25]Robert L. Sterdivant, from Monrovia, August 14, 1857, to Salley C. Brent, deposit, Cocke Papers, quoted in *Ibid.*, pp. 83-84.

[26]James P. Skipwith, from Monrovia, August 20, 1859, to John H. Cocke, deposit, Cocke Papers, quoted in *Ibid.*, p. 93.

[27]Washington W. McDonogh, from King Will's Town, October 7, 1846, to John McDonogh, deposit, McDonogh Papers, quoted in *Ibid.*, pp. 141-142.

[28]A. Jackson, from Monrovia, November 11, 1846, to John McDonogh, deposit, McDonogh Papers, quoted in *Ibid.*, pp. 143-144.

[29]For the details, see *Ibid.*, and Miller, ed. *Dear Masters.*

[30]Johnston, *Liberia*, p. 390.

[31]W. V. S. Tubman, who became Liberia's President in 1944, succeeded in enlarging the indigenous "civilized Liberian community." This was mainly carried out to create an alternative political base. Such a strategy was essential for Tubman's political survival, for he was not from Monrovia, the main center of power in Liberia. Despite this, Tubman was careful not to undermine the immigrant Liberian elite class to which he also belonged. This explained why the indigenous Liberians who were accepted as "civilized" and were politically, economically, and socially rewarded for this, were not allowed to challenge the class supremacy of the immigrant Liberians. Those who attempted to do so, or had the potential for doing so, were expelled and punished. For the details of this argument, see the following works: Hlophe, *Class Ethnicity, and Politics in Liberia*; Nimley, *The Liberian Bureaucracy*; Fraenkel, *Tribe and Class in Monrovia*; Gus Liebenow, *The Evolution of Privilege* (Ithaca, 1969); and Lowenkopf, *Politics in Liberia*.

[33]*Ibid.*

[34]*Ibid.*

[35]This statement was made by President W. R. Tolbert a few days after the rice riot in Monrovia that almost overthrew him in April, 1979.

For details of this emphasis, see Holloway's *Liberian Diplomacy in Africa*, pp. 153-178.

[36]This view is inferred from Scott Nearing's *Beyond Civilization and Learning from History* (Harborside, 1975), pp. XX-XIV.

[37]West, *Back to Africa*, p. 327.

CONCLUSION

This study has been an attempt to analyze the historical development of nineteenth-century Liberia. It provides an exposition of the main forces which shaped the West African nation during that period and, indeed, even later. The ACS was by far the most influential force. Although not the only factor which influenced the political, economic, and social shape of Liberia, the impact of the ACS was clearly enormous, and it must be seen as a major determinant force in the historical development of Liberia.

While it is argued that both the ACS and pre-Liberian African society played crucial roles in that development, the effects of the former became predominant. As treated in Chapters III through VI, Liberia's main social formations, such as its political, economic, and religious institutional developments, were largely called into being by the ACS. Paternalism, which enhanced the development of political, economic, and other social formations in Liberia, for example, was introduced in that country by the ACS.

An important example of the political culture of paternalism was that only those settlers who closely identified or eloquently articulated the values inherent in the ACS were destined to be leaders in the Liberian settlement. Their power was not only limited to political leadership; it also extended to include the administering of every key Liberian social institution. This explains why those who became leaders, especially the ones appointed to top positions, were not only politically powerful, but they were also economically and socially influential.

This was made possible, in the first instance, by the fact that items such as food, building materials, clothing, educational facilities, and agricultural utensils made available to the settlers were first put into the care of the top leaders who were headed by the governor, the chief representative of the ACS in the settlement. As detailed in the study, these materials were distributed by the governor and his close assistants. The method of distribution of the items in question was paternalistically designed to guarantee perpetually the authority of the governor. Those who closely identified with the various institutional values the governor was encouraged by the ACS to promote in Liberia were the most rewarded. Those who did not were disliked and were occasionally punished. Taking into consideration the reality of the Liberian settlement, most of the early settlers had few alternatives but to conform to the social standards set by the ACS through its governors. It could, therefore, be reasonably maintained that the social culture of paternalism was employed in Liberia as a means of social control. Of course, this was identical with the paternalism practiced by most of the eminent members of the ACS in administering their slaves in the Old South.

The fact that paternalism was introduced in Liberia as an influential social force meant that it was to have a lasting impact on that country. With no doubt, there were other factors that enhanced its development as a complex political, economic, and social system in Liberia. These factors included the social reality of the area that became Liberia, the role of the world economic system, and the activities of the different western nations.

Beginning with the first factor, the area of the pre-Liberian coast, as examined in Chapter II, had already been stratified and reoriented to meet the requirements of the oceanic slave trade before the arrival of the Americans. The members of the top layer of the stratification became the new coastal elites. They had gained their new status by grossly exploiting both the natural and human resources of the region. But the advance of the American settlers posed a serious threat to the new social establishment. This development was a direct result of the fact that the advance was also associated with the crusade to stop the oceanic slave trade by destroying its main source of supply. No wonder the new coastal elites, especially those who were abundantly benefiting from the slave trade, became increasingly hostile to the American settlers. As implied in Chapter III, this hostile attitude toward the American settlers only reinforced the conditions that called for their acquiescence in the various values that the ACS was trying to encourage them to accept.

Pertinent to this argument is the fact that the commercial progress of the various European powers on the coast of pre-, colonial, and independent Liberia only added to the situations that were demanding that the settlers accept the social culture of paternalism and the other institutional values introduced by the ACS if they were to survive politically. This was more so since the commercial advance came to threaten the sovereignty of Liberia. This explains why most of the settlers, especially during the early independent era, accepted the new social arrangements without much protest. This trend was further enhanced by the new elites' successful evocation of the nationalistic sentiment of the Liberian settlers. While this helped to rally the settlers against the European advance, at the same time it helped to allay the internal opposition to the social array of Liberia. Abatement of opposition to the new social arrangements was indeed a victory for the Liberian elites since it helped them to secure their hegemony. This, of course, meant the continuation of the system and values that had been introduced in Liberia by the ACS.

But these circumstances were not the only forces that helped with the perpetuation of the various institutional values in question. In fact, these values differed little from those inherent in the nineteenth-century world economic system. Thus, that system helped to reinforce the foregoing institutional arrangements. Despite the fact that the world economy subordinated the Liberian elites, it did not destroy their political and social supremacy in Liberia. In fact, it enhanced their continued domination. This was made possible by the fact that the relatively minimal gain the elites made from their ancillary participation in the system was invested in ways which facilitated their social domination. This explains why political and economic power during the period under consideration continued to be largely concentrated in the hands of these elites. But who would reasonably argue that this was not in concurrence with the social arrangements introduced in Liberia by the ACS and the resulting performance of the economic system with which the elites were subordinately involved? In other words, Liberia's social arrangements and the world economic system had certain things in common, despite the fact that the former was subordinated by the latter. It is not surprising that they continued to enhance each other's development though this process was not always harmonious.

The roles of the different western churches in Liberia also served as reinforcers of that country's institutional developments. Their great emphasis on Christian doctrines and values in Liberia only reinforced the concept strongly promoted by the ACS that not only was the Liberian entity God's creation, but the failures and achievements of that country were also divinely predetermined. Although this was in harmony with the ACS' religious stress and it helped to preserve the hegemony of the Liberian elites, such a religious emphasis only reinforced the impotence of the elites to treat critically the various social problems their country was confronting. This made it easy to accept failure since their shortcomings were easily attributed to Providence. No wonder even their concept of a civilized society was defined in a Christian context.

It may thus be concluded that Liberia's key institutional values were largely and fundamentally extensions of those that were inherent in the ACS, despite the fact that they were shaped by the different forces examined in the study. The continuation of the ACS' social, political, economic, and religious paternalism in its exemplified form of extreme monopolizations of nearly all Liberia's main institutional powers by the elites of that country during the period covered bears testimony to this. Indisputably, this kind of social arrangement was not free from violent opposition. The major revolts against it in 1823, 1871, 1980, and again in 1985 eloquently sustain this. But once again, these developments, like most of Liberia's past and present critical political, social, and economic problems, cannot be fully understood without tracing them to their historical source, the ACS.

APPENDIX

Administrative Leaders of Liberia, 1819-1900

Chief Administrator of the ACS/Governor

Eli Ayres, 1821-1824
Jehudi Ashmun, 1824-1828
Joseph Mechlin, Jr., 1829-1833
John P. Pinney, 1833-1835
Ezekiel Skinner, 1835-1836
Anthony D. Williams, 1836-1839
Thomas Buchanan, 1839-1841
Joseph J. Roberts, 1841-1847

Presidents of Liberia

Joseph J. Roberts, 1847-1856
Stephen A. Benson, 1856-1864
Daniel B. Warner, 1864-1868
James S. Payne, 1868-1870
Edward J. Roye, 1870-1871
James S. Smith, 1871-1872
Joseph J. Roberts 1872-1876
James S. Payne, 1876-1878
Anthony W. Gardner, 1878-1883
Alfred H. Russell, 1883-1892
Hilary R. W. Johnson, 1883-1892
Joseph J. Cheeseman, 1892-1896
William D. Coleman, 1896-1900

SELECT BIBLIOGRAPHY

Biographical Note

The basic sources for this study have been the publications of the ACS (the *African Repository* and the *Annual Reports*), archival and other government documents and publications, primary accounts, private correspondence between Liberian settlers and their relatives and former masters in the United States, and relevant secondary works.

For a study of this kind, the importance of the *African Repository* and the *Annual Reports* of the ACS should not be underestimated. The reasons for this are well known to scholars who have studied the ACS. The *Annual Reports*, which began publication in 1818, and the *African Repository*, initiated in 1823, continued to be the official organs of the ACS up to 1894. These sources, especially the latter, contained among other things, ACS' annual reports, information about activities of the body in the United States and Liberia, reports and correspondence of church and secular leaders who were directly or indirectly involved with the ACS, and reports of American naval officials who visited Liberia. Included in these sources are also lists of names of the Americans who emigrated to Liberia, the ships they sailed on, and letters written by them. One does not find these sources, however, critical of the ACS. This explains why the works of critics such as Jay, Stuart, Ruffin, and Stebbins are used to provide alternative views of ACS' activities in Liberia.

Other primary sources which must be mentioned are Liberian archival holdings. Although most are in the custody of the Liberian Ministry of Foreign Affairs, some of the holdings are in the care of the Ministry of Information and Cultural Affairs and a semi-autonomousbody known as the National DocumentationCenter. These are all located in Monrovia, though not in the same building. This arrangement makes it difficult for one to have an easy access to the documents. In addition to this problem, the materials are poorly organized. Most have no file numbers which might serve as easy reference for scholars. The documents consulted are listed here under the heading Liberian National Archives rather than by location.

The archival holdings in Liberia include early government publications, correspondence of the key representatives of the ACS in colonial Liberia, correspondence of the leaders of independent Liberia, miscellaneous documents dealing with such issues as foreign relations, legal problems, legislative records, and educational and religious problems. Fortunately, many of these materials were reprinted in the *Annual Report* or the *African Repository*.

Also relevant to this study is the correspondence of the ordinary settlers. Fortunately, many of the letters written by these individuals have been edited and published by Wiley and Miller. Another primary source of importance to this study which should be noted is Gurley's biography of Ashmun. This work is not only about Ashmun's activities in Liberia; it also deals, though not critically, with the early economic, political, and social development of Liberia.

Archival materials or government sources dealing mainly with the American aspect of the ACS were not exhausted for two main reasons: first these materials have been examined by works previously done on the American aspect of the ACS. Second, this work mainly deals with the ACS impact on Liberia's institutional developments. Thus while American archival sources were not extensively investigated, scholarly works on the ACS and nineteenth century Liberia which are most relevant to the study were consulted. These works are listed on the succeeding pages.

Primary Sources

Archival Collections

Charlottesville, Virginia. University of Virginia Library: Cocke Family Papers; McDonogh Papers.

Chicago, Illinois. Chicago Historical Society: American Colonization Society Papers; Joseph Jenkins Roberts Papers.

Monrovia, Liberia. Liberian National Archives:
Colonial Council Minutes, 1838-1839.
Commonwealth Court Records, 1838-1847.
Commonwealth Legislative Minutes, 1837-1847.
Correspondence of Colonial Agents, 1833-1841.
Dannis, Gabriel L. Brief Outline of Liberia-German Relations.
Deed Records, Montserrado County, 1847.
Department of Justice Correspondence, 1892-1904.
Executive Mansion Journal of H. R. W. Johnson, 1885-1888.
Jehudi Ashmun Papers, 1826-1828.
Miscellaneous State Department Correspondence.
Minutes of the Court of Quarter Sessions and Common Pleas.
Minutes of the Monthly and Probate Court, Montserrado County, 1847-1877.
Minutes of the Senate, 1849-1892.
State Department Correspondence, Foreign and Local, 1886- 1906.
True Whig National Convention, 1869.

Monrovia, Liberia. University of Liberia Library: Jesse and Mars Lucas Correspondence.

Morgantown, West Virginia. West Virginia and Regional History Collection: Journal of John Moore McCalla, 1860.

Washington, D. C. Library of Congress Manuscript Division: American Colonization Society Papers.

Washington, D. C. U. S. National Archives: Microcopy 169, Despatches from the United States Consuls in Monrovia, 1852-1906.

Washington, D. C. U. S. National Archives: Microcopy 170, Despatches from the United States to Liberia, 1863-1906.

Government Publications

Republic of Liberia

Constitution of the Republic of Liberia (Monrovia, 1847).

The Declaration of Independence of Liberia (Monrovia, 1847).

Treaties and Conventions Concluded Between Liberia and Foreign Powers, 1847-1907 (Monrovia, 1907).

United States Government

United States Congress, House of Representatives. *Report of John Seys, 1856-1863.* House Executive Document No. 28, 37th Congress, 3rd Session, 1863.

______. *Report of the Reverend R. R. Gurley.* House Executive Document No. 75, 31st Congress, 1st Session, 1849-1850.

United States Congress, Senate. *Tables Showing the Number of Emigrants and Recaptured Africans Sent to the Colony of Liberia--by the Government of the United States. . . .* Senate Document No. 150, 28th Congress, 2nd Session, 1845.

Books

Alexander, Archibald. *A History of Colonization on the Western Coast of Africa.* Philadelphia: W. S. Martien, 1846.

American Colonization Society Bulletin in Liberia. Washington: 1853.

American Colonization Society Bulletin in Liberia. Washington: 1895.

Anderson, Benjamin J. *Narrative of Journey to Musardu: The Capital of the Western Mandingoes. . . .* 2nd Edition. London: Frank Cass, 1971.

Ashmun, Jehudi. *History of the American Colony of Liberia from the Authentic Records of the Colony.* Washington: Day and Gideon, 1826.

______. *Memoir . . . of the Rev. Samuel Bacon. . . .* Washington: J. Gideon Jr., 1822.

Atkins, John. *A Voyage to Guinea, Brasil, and the West Indies.* London: Hakluyt Society, 1735.

The Baptist General Convention, Fifth Triennial Proceedings. 1826.

Ball, S. S. *Liberia: The Conditions and Prospects of the Republic.* Alton, 1848.

Barbot, John. *A Description of the Coasts of North and South Guinea.* London: Hakluyt Society, 1794.

Beaver, Philip. *African Memoranda Relative to an Attempt to Establish a British Settlement on the Island of Bolama in the Year 1792.* London: Hakluyt Society, 1805.

Blake, J. W. *Europeans in West Africa, 1450-1560.* London: Hakluyt Society, 1742.

Bosman, W. *A New and Accurate Description of the Coast of Guinea.* Reprint. London: Ballantyne Press, 1907.

Constitution, Government, and Digest of the Laws of Liberia as Confirmed and Established by the Board of Managers of the American Colonization Society. Washington: 1825.

Corry, Joseph. *Observation Upon the Windward Coast of Africa and the Religion, Character, Customs of the Natives.* London: Hakluyt Society, 1807.

Cornish, Samuel E. and Wright, Theodore S. *The Colonization Scheme.* Newark: State Printer, 1840.

Cowan, Alexander. *Liberia As I found It in 1858.* Lexington: A. G. Hodges, 1858.

Cowley, Malcolm, ed. *Adventures of an African Slaver: Being a True Account of the Life of Captain Theodore Canot.* Cleveland: World Publishing Company, 1942.

Crumwell, Alexander. *The Future of Africa.* New York: C. Scribner, 1862.

______. *The Duty of a Rising Christian State.* London: Werthelin and MacIntosh, 1858.

Gurley, Ralph Randolph. *Letter to . . . On the Colonization and Civilization of Africa.* London: Wiley & Putnam, 1841.

______. *Mission to England on Behalf of the American Colonization Society.* Washington: J. C. Dunn, 1840.

______. *Life of Jehudi Ashmun.* Washington: J. C. Dunn, 1835.

Hodkins, Thomas. *An Inquiry into the Merits of the American Colonization Society and Reply to the Charges Brought Against It with an Account of the British Colonization Society.* London: J. and A. Arch Cornhill, 1833.

Jay, William. *An Inquiry into the Character and Tendency of the American Colonization and American Anti-Slavery Societies.* Reprint. New York: Kraus Reprint Company, 1969.

Laing, A. G. *Travels in the Timannee, Kooranko and Soolima Countries.* London: Hakluyt Society, 1825.

Miller, Randall M., ed. *Dear Master: Letters of a Slave Family.* Ithaca: Cornell University Press, 1976.

Stebbins, G. B. *Facts and Opinions Touching the Real Origin, Character, and Influence of the American Colonization Society:. . . .* Boston: John P. Jewell and Company, 1853.

A View of Exertions Lately Made for the Purpose of Colonizing the Free People of Color in Africa or Elsewhere. Washington: 1817.

Wiley, Bell I., ed. *Letters From Liberia, 1833-1869.* Lexington: University of Kentucky Press, 1980.

Newspapers and Journals

African Observer (Monrovia), 1826-1828.
Africa's Luminary (Monrovia).
Annual Report of the American Colonization Society. (Washington), 1818-1910.
African Repository and Colonial Journal (Washington), 1825-1900.
Liberia Herald (Monrovia), 1823-
Liberia Recorder, (Monrovia).
The Observer.
Radical Abolitionist (United States), 1855-1858.
Weekly Afro-American (New York).

Secondary Sources

Ajayi, Ade J. and Espie, Ian, eds. *A Thousand Years of West African History.* Ibadan University Press, 1965.

Akpan, M. B. "Black Imperialism: Americo-LiberianRule Over the African People of Liberia, 1822-1964," *Canadian Journal of African Studies*, VII, No. 2 (1973).

Amin, Samir. *Imperialism and Unequal Development.* New York: Monthly Review Press, 1977.

______. *Unequal Development*. New York: Monthly Review Press, 1976.

______. *Accumulation on a World Scale*. New York: Monthly Review Press, 1974.

______. *Neo-Colonialism in West Africa*. New York: Monthly Review Press, 1973.

Andrews, Kenneth R. *Trade, Plunder and Settlement: Maritime Enterprises and the Genesis of the British Empire, 14801630*. Cambridge: Cambridge University Press, 1984.

Anene, C. J. and Brown, G. N., eds. *Africa in the Nineteenth and Twentieth Centuries*. Ibadan: Ibadan University Press, 1966.

Aptheker, Herbert. *The Nature of Democracy, Freedom and Revolution*. New York: International Publishers, 1975.

Arghiri, Emmanuel. *Unequal Exchange*. New York: Monthly Review Press, 1972.

Azikiwe, Nnamdi. *The Future of Pan-Africanism*. Lagos: Daily Times, 1964.

______. *Liberia in World Politics*. London: A. H. Stockwell, 1934.

Bakir, Abd el-Mohsen. *Slavery in Pharaonic Egypt*. Cairo: George Routledge & Sons, 1952.

Battle, Vincent and Charles H. Lyons, eds. *Essays in the History of African Education*. New York: Teachers College Press, 1980.

Beaud, Michael. *A History of Capitalism 1500-1980*. New York: Monthly Review Press, 1983.

Berlin, Ira. *Slaves Without Masters: The Free Negro in the Antebellum South*. New York: Pantheon Books, 1974.

Betts, F. Raymond. *The Scramble for Africa*. Lexington: D. C. Heath and Company, 1966.

Blassingame, John W. *The Slave community: Plantation Life in the Antebellum South*. New York: Oxford University Press, 1974.

Blyden, Edward Wilmont. *Christianity, Islam, and the Negro Race*. London: W. B. Whittingham and Company, 1888.

______. *On Mixed Races in Liberia*. Washington: Smithsonian Institution, 1870.

______. *Liberia's Offering*. New York: John A. Gray, 1862.

Boxer, C. R. *Four Centuries of Portuguese Expansion, 1415-1825*. Los Angeles: University of California Press, 1969.

Brown, George W. *The Economic History of Liberia*. Washington: The Associated Publishers, 1941.

Browne, George D. "History of the Protestant Episcopal Mission in Liberia up to 1838, *Historical Magazine of the Protestant Episcopal Church, VI,* No. 1 (1970).

Bruce, P. A. *Economic History of Virginia in the Nineteenth Century*. Vol. II. New York: P. Smith, 1896.

Buckland, William W. *Roman Law of Slavery: The Conditions of Slaves in Private Law From Augustus to Justinian*. Cambridge: Cambridge University Press, 1908.

Buell, Raymond L. *The Native Problem in Africa*. Vol. II. New York: The Macmillan Company, 1928.

Campbell, Penelope. *Maryland in Africa: The Maryland State Colonization Society, 1831-1857*. Urbana: University of Illinois Press, 1971.

Cardoso, Fernandez and Enzo Faletto. *Dependency and Development in Latin America*. Los Angeles: University of California Press, 1979.

Carrington, C. E. *The British Overseas: Exploits of a Nation of Shopkeepers*. London: Cambridge University Press, 1968.

Cash, W. J. *The Mind of the South*. New York: Vintage Books, 1960.

Cipolla, Carlo. *Guns, Sails, and Empires: Technological Innovation and the Early Phases of European Expansion, 1400-1700*. New York: Pantheon Books, 1965.

Coleman, James. *Slavery Times in Kentucky*. Chapel Hill: University of North Carolina Press, 1940.

Communings, John. *Negro Population in the United States, 1790- 1915*. Washington: Associated Press, 1918.

Cook, Jacob, ed. *Frederic Bancroft, Historian*. Norman: University Press of Oklahoma, 1967.

Cornforth, Maurice. *Historical Materialism*. New York: Monthly Review Press, 1977.

Crowder, Michael, ed. *West African Resistance*. Ife: Ibadan University Press, 1970.

Curties, Merle. *The Social Ideas of American Educators*. New York: Doubleday, Doran and Company, 1935.

Curtin, Philip. *Economic Change in Pre-colonial Africa: Senegambia in the Era of the Slave Trade*. Madison: University of Madison Press, 1975.

______. *The Atlantic Slave Trade: A Census*. Madison: University of Wisconsin Press, 1969.

_____. *The Image of Africa: British Ideas and Action, 1780-1850.* London: Macmillan and Company, 1965.

Dalton, George. "History and Economic Development in Liberia," *Journal of Economic History*, XXV (1965).

Davidson, Basil. *Black Mother.* Boston: Gallance, 1960.

Davies, K. G. *The Royal African Company.* London: Longmans, 1957.

Davis, David Brion. *Slavery and Human Progress.* New York: Oxford University Press, 1984.

_____. *The Problem of Slavery in the Age of Revolution, 1770-1823.* Ithaca: Cornell University Press, 1975.

_____. *The Problem of Slavery in Western Culture.* Ithaca: Cornell University Press, 1967.

Davis, Ronald W. *Ethnohistorical Studies on the Kru Coast.* Newark: The Institute of Liberian Studies, 1976.

_____. "Historical Outline of the Kru Coast, Liberia, 1500 to the Present," Ph.D. Dissertation, Indiana University, 1968.

De La Rue, Sidney. *The Land of the Pepper Bird.* New York: G. P. Putnam's Son, 1930.

Draper, Theodore. *The Rediscovery of Black Nationalism.* New York: Viking Press, 1970.

DuBois, W. E. B. *Black Reconstruction in America.* New York: Harcourt Brace and Company, 1935.

_____. "Liberia and Rubber" *New Republic* (1925).

_____. *The Souls of Black Folks.* Chicago: A. C. MacClung, 1903.

Dunn, Richard S. *Sugar and Slaves: Rise of the Planter Class in the English West Indies, 1624-1713*. Chapel Hill: University of North Carolina Press, 1971.

Durham, Frederick Alexander. *The Lone Star of Liberia*. London: E. Stock, 1892.

Ellis, George W. *Negro Culture in West Africa*. New York: Neal Publishing Company, 1914.

Fage, John D. *A History of Africa*. New York: Alfred A. Knopf, 1978.

______. "Slavery and the Slave Trade in the Context of West African History," *Journal of African History*, X, No. 3 (1969).

Finley, M. I. *Ancient Slavery and Modern Ideology*. New York: Penguin Books, 1980.

Fitzhugh, George. *Sociology for the South or the Failure of Free Society*. Richmond: A. Morries, 1854.

Ford, Paul L. *The Writings of Thomas Jefferson*. Vol. III. New York: Putnam and Company, 1905.

Ford, Worthington C. *The Writings of George Washington*. New York: Putnam's Sons, 1893.

Fordes, E. A. *The Land of the White Helmet: Lights and Shadows Across Africa*. New York: Fleming H. Revell Company, 1926.

Foster, Charles I. "The Colonization of Free Negroes is Liberia, 1816-1835," *Journal of Negro History*, XXXXVIII, (1953).

Fox, Early. *The American Colonization Society, 1817-1840*. Baltimore: Johns Hopkins University Press, 1919.

Fraenkel, M. "Social Change on the Kru Coast of Liberia," *Africa*, XXXVI (1966).

Fraenkel, M. "Social Change on the Kru Coast of Liberia," *Africa*, XXXVI (1966).

______. *Tribe and Class in Monrovia*. London: Oxford University Press, 1964.

Freeman, Frederick. *Yaradee: A Plea for Africa in Familiar Conversations on the Subject of Slavery and Colonization*. Philadelphia: J. Whiteman, 1836.

Freeman, M. H. "The Education Wants of the Free Colored People," *Anglo-American Magazine* (1858).

Fyfe, Christopher. *Sierra Leone Inheritance*. Oxford: Oxford University Press, 1964.

______. *A History of Sierra Leone*. London: Oxford University Press, 1962.

Galevano, Eduardo. *Open Veins of Latin America: Five Centuries of Pillage of a Continent*. New York: Monthly Review Press, 1973.

Garrison, William L . *Thoughts on the African Colonization. . . .* Boston: Garrison and Knapp, 1832.

Garvey, Marcus. *Philosophy and Opinions*. 2 Vols. New York: Universal Publishing House, 1926.

Genovese, Elizabeth and Genovese, Eugene D. *Fruits of Merchant Capital: Slavery and Bourgeois Property in the Rise and Expansion of Capitalism*. New York: Oxford University Press, 1983.

Genovese, Eugene D. *The World The Slaveholders Made*. New York: Vintage: Vintage Books, 1971.

______. *Political Economy of Slavery: Studies in the Economy and Society of the Slave South*. New York: Vintage Books, 1967.

Gordon, Donald C. *The Movement of Power: Britain's Imperial Epoch.* London: Prentice Hall, 1970.

Gray, John. *The History of Gambia*. Cambridge: Cambridge University Press, 1940.

Greenberg, Joseph. *The Languages of Africa*. Bloomington: Indiana University Press, 1964.

Griffith, Cyril E. "Martin R. Delany and the African Dream, 1812-1835," Ph.D. Dissertation, Michigan State University, 1973.

Hale, Sarah. *Liberia: Or Mr. Lyton's Experiments*. New York: Harper and Brothers, 1853.

Haliburton, Gordon. "The Prophet Harries and His Work in Ivory Coast and Western Ghana," Ph.D. Dissertation, University of London, 1967.

Hargreaves, John. "Liberia: The Price of Independence," *Odu: A Journal of West African Studies*, No. 6 (1972).

Harris, Sheldon H. *Paul Cuffee Black American and the African Return.* New York: Simon and Schuster, 1972.

Henries, Dories Banks. *The Liberian Nation: A Short History.* London: Macmillan and Company, 1967.

______. *The Life of Joseph Jenkins Roberts and His Inaugural Addresses.* London: Macmillan and Company, 1964.

Hill, Adelaide C. and Kilson, Martin, eds. *Apropos of Africa*. London: Frank Cass, 1969.

Hill, K. Q., ed. *Towards a New Strategy for Development.* New York: Pergamon Press, 1977.

Hlophe, Stephen S. *Class, Ethnicity and Politics in Liberia: A Class Analysis of Power Struggles in the Tubman and Tolbert*

Administrations From 1944-1975. Washington: University Press of America, 1979.

Hofstadter, Richard. *Social Darwinism in American Thought*. Boston: Beacon Press, 1977.

Holloway, Joseph E. *Liberian Diplomacy in Africa: A Study in Inter-African Relations*. Washington: University Press of America, 1981.

Holsoe, Sevend. "Economic Activities in the Liberia Area: The Pre-European Period to 1900," *Liberian Studies Series*, No. 6 (1979).

_____. "The Cassava-Leaf People: An Ethno-historical Study of the Vai People with Particular Emphasis on the Tervo Chiefdom," Ph.D. Dissertation, Boston University, 1967.

Huberich, Charles Henry. *The Political and Legislative History of Liberia*: . . . 2 Vols. New York: Central Book Company, 1947.

Huggins, Nathan. *Black Odyssey: The Afro-American Ordeal in Slavery*. New York: Pantheon Books, 1977.

Hunt, Gaillard, ed. *The Writings of James Madison*. Vol. III. New York: Putnam's Sons, 1910.

Jackson, Luther P. *Free Negro Labor and Property Holding in Virginia, 1830-1860*. New York: Appleton-Century Co., 1942.

_____. "Free Negroes of Petersburg, Virginia," *Journal of Negro History*, I (1916).

Jenkins, William. *Pro-Slavery Thought in the Old South*. Chapel Hill: University of North Carolina Press, 1935.

Jernegan, Marcus W. *Laboring and Dependent Classes in Colonial America, 1607-1783*. Chicago: University of Chicago Press, 1931.

______. "Slavery and Conversion in the American Colonies," American Historical Review, XXI (1916).

John, John. *A Memoir of the Life of the Right Reverend William Meade.* Richmond: n.d.

Johnson, Michael P. and Roark, James L. *Black Masters: A Free Family of Color in the South.* New York: W. W. Norton and Company, 1984.

Johnston, Harry. *Liberia.* Vol. II. New York: Dodd and Company, 1906.

Jones, Hannah A. B. "The Struggle for Political and Cultural Unification in Liberia, 1847-1937," Ph.D. Dissertation, Northwestern University, 1962.

Jordan, Winthrop D. *The Whiteman's Burden: Historical Origins of Racism in the United States.* New York: Oxford University Press, 1974.

______. *White Over Black: American Attitudes Toward the Negro, 1550-1812.* Chapel Hill: University of North Carolina Press, 1971.

Kamenka, Eugene. *Marxism and Ethics.* London: Macmillan and Company, 1970.

Karnga, A. *A Guide to Our Criminal and Civil Procedure.* Liverpool: D. H. Tyte and Company, 1926.

______. *History of Liberia.* Liberpool: D. H. Tyte and Company, 1926.

______. *Liberia Before the New World.* London: W. Blackwood and Sons, 1923.

Kingsley, Mary. *Travels in West Africa.* London: Macmillan and Company, 1897.

Knight, Franklin W. *Slave Society in Cuba in the Nineteenth Century.* Madison: University of Wisconsin Press, 1970.

Kreps, Peter. *Sierra Leone, 1400-1787*. Cambridge: Cambridge University Press, 1967.

Legum, Colin. *Pan-Africanism: A Short Political Guide*. London: Pall Mall, 1962.

Lenin, V. I. *Imperialism: The Highest Stage of Capitalism*. New York: International Publishers, 1939.

Lens, Sidney. *The Forging of the American Empire: A History of American Imperialism From the Revolution to Vietnam*. New York: Thomas J. Crowell Company, 1974.

Liebenow, Gus. *Liberia: The Evolution of Privilege*. Ithaca: Cornell University Press, 1969.

Litwack, Leon. *North of Slavery: The Negro in the Free States, 1790-1860*. Chicago: University of Chicago Press, 1961.

Livermore, George. *An Historical Research Respecting the Opinions of the Founding Fathers of the Republic on the Negroes as Slaves, as Citizens, and as Soldiers*. Boston: J. Wilson and Son, 1862.

Lowenkopf, Martin. *Politics in Liberia: The Conservative Road to Development*. Stanford: Hoover Institution Press, 1976.

Lynch, Hollis. *Edward Wilmont Blyden: Pan-Negro Patriot, 1832-1912*. London: Oxford University Press, 1964.

MacIver, Robert. *Politics and Society*. New York: Atherton Press, 1966.

Magdoff, Harry and Sweezy, Paul M. *The End of Prosperity: The American Economy in the 1970s*. New York: Monthly Review Press 1977.

Mandel, Ernest and Novack, George. *Late Capitalism*. London: Redwood Burn Ltd., 1980.

______. *The Marxist Theory of Alienation*. New York: Pathfinder Press 1970.

Mannix, Daniel and Cowley, Malcolm. *Black Cargoes: A History of the Atlantic Slave Trade, 1518-1865*. New York: The Viking Press, 1962.

Martin, Jane. "The Dual Legacy: Government Authority and Mission Influence Among the Glebo of Eastern Liberia, 1834-1910," Ph.D. Dissertation, Boston University, 1968.

Martin, B. and Supurrell, M., eds. Newton, John. *Thought Upon the African Trade, 1750-1754*. London: Epworth Press, 1962.

Martin, E., ed. Owen, Nicholas. *Journal of a Slave Dealer on the Coast of Africa and America From 1746 to the Year 1757*. London Epworth Press, 1964.

Maugham, R. F. *Republic of Liberia*. London: G. Allen and Unwin, 1920.

McEvoy, Frederick. "History, Tradition, and Kinship as Factors in Modern Labor Migration," Ph.D. Dissertation, University of London, 1956.

McPhee, Allen. *The Economic Revolution of British West Africa*. London: Routledge and Sons, 1926.

McPherson, T. *A History of Liberia*. Baltimore: Johns Hopkins University Press, 1891.

Mehlinger, L. R. "The Attitude of the Free Negro Towards African Colonization," *Journal of Negro History*, I (1916).

Mellon, Matthew. *Early American Views on Negro Slavery: From the Letters and Papers of the Founders of the Republic*. New York: Pergamon Publishers, 1934.

Miers, Suzanne and Kopytoff, Igor, eds. *Slavery in Africa: Historical and Anthropological Perspectives*. Madison: University of Wisconsin Press, 1977.

Miller, A. M. "Import Trade of London, 1600-1640," Ph.D. Dissertation, University of London, 1956.

Mills, Dorothy. *Through Liberia*. New York: Frederick A. Stokes Company, n.d.

Mittleman, James. *Underdevelopment and the Transition to Socialism: Mozambique and Tanzania*. New York: Academic Press, 1981.

Morison, Samuel, Henry Commager and William Leuchtenburg. *A Concise History of the American Republic*. Oxford: Oxford University Press, 1983.

Morgan, Edmund. *American Freedom, American Slavery*. New York: Norton, 1975.

______. "Slavery and Freedom: The American Paradox," *Journal of American History*, LIX (1972).

Morrow, Glenn. *Plato's Law of Slavery in Relation to Greek Law*. Urbana: University of Illinois Press, 1938.

Nash, Gary. *Red, White, Black: The Peoples of Early America*. Englewood Cliffs: Prentice Hall Inc., 1974.

Nash, Gerald, ed. *Issues in American Economic History*. Boston: D. C. Heath Company, 1964.

Nimley, J. Anthony. *The Liberian Bureaucracy: An Analysis and Evaluation of the Environment, Structure and Function*. Washington: University Press of America, 1977.

Nkrumah, Kwame. *Africa Must Unite*. Accra: Heinemann, 1963.

Oakes, James. *The Ruling Race: A History of American Slaveholders*. New York: Random House, 1983.

Onimode, Bade. *Imperialism and Underdevelopment in Nigeria*. London: Zed Press, 1982.

Opper, Kent. "The Minds of White Participants in the African Colonization Movement, 1816-1840," Ph.D. Dissertation, University of North Carolina, 1972.

O'Sullivan, John and Deuchel, Edward F. *American Economic History: From Abundance to Constraint*. New York: Franklin Watts, 1981.

Padmore, George. *Pan-Africanism or Communism?* London: Dennis Dobson, 1956.

Palmer, Robert. *The Age of the Democratic Revolution: A Political History of Europe and America, 1760-1800*. Princeton: Princeton University Press, 1959.

Parry, J. H. *The Establishment of European Hegemony: Trade and Exploration in the Age of the Renaissance, 1415-1715*. New York: Harper Torchbooks, 1966.

Pennsylvania Anti-Slavery Society, *Address to the Coloured People of the State of Pennsylvania*. Philadelphia: 1837.

Person, Yves. "Des Kru en Haute-Volta," *Bulletin de l'Institute Francais Afrique Noire*, XXVIII (1966).

Phillips, Ulrich. *American Negro Slavery*. Baton Rouge: Louisiana State University Press, 1918.

Polanyi, K. "Sortings and Ounce Trade in the West African Slave Trade," *Journal of African History*, V, No. 3 (1964).

Potholm, Christian. *Theory and Practice of African Politics*. Englewood Cliffs: Prentice-Hall, 1979.

Roberts, Joseph. *The Republic of Liberia*. Washington: Colonial Society Building, 1869.

Robinson, Cedric. *Black Marxism: The Making of the Black Radical Tradition*. London: 3rd Press, 1983.

Rodney, Walter. *A History of the Upper Guinea Coast, 1545-1800*. Oxford: Clarendon Press, 1971.

______. "A Reconsiderationof the Mane Invasion of Sierra Leone," *Journal of African History*, VIII (1967).

______. "African Slavery and Other Forms of Social Oppression on the Upper Guinea Coast in the Context of the Atlantic Slave Trade," *Journal of African History*, VII (1966).

Rotberg, Robert and Kilson, Martin, eds. *Africa Diaspora: Interpretative Essays*. Cambridge: Cambridge University Press, 1976.

Ruchames, Louis, ed. *Racial Thought in America From the Puritans to Abraham Lincoln*. Amherst: Universityof MassachusettsPress, 1969.

Ruffin, Edmund. *American Colonization Unveiled*. Date and Place unknown.

Schlaifer, Robert. "Greek Theories of Slavery from Homer to Aristotle," *Harvard Studies in Classical Philology*, XLVII (1936).

Seifmnam, Eli. "A History of the New York Colonization Society," Ph.D. Dissertation, New York University, 1965.

Sherwood, Henry Noble. "Early Negro Deportation Projects," *Mississippi Valley Historical Review*, II, No. 4 (1916).

______. "Paul Cuffee and His Contribution to the American Colonization Society," *Proceedingsof the Mississippi Valley HistoricalAssociation*, VI (1912).

______. "The Formation of the American Colonization Society," *Journal of Negro History*, 1911.

Shick, Tom. *Behold the Promised Land: A History of Afro-American Settler Society in Nineteenth Century Liberia*. Baltimore: Johns Hopkins University Press, 1980.

______. "The Social and Economic History of Afro-American Settlers in Liberia, 1820-1900," Ph.D. Dissertation, University of Wisconsin, 1976.

______. "A Quantitative Analysis of Liberian Colonization from 1820 to 1843 with Special Reference to Mortality," *Journal of African History*, XII, No. 1 (1971).

Sigler, Phil. "Attitudes of the Free Blacks Towards Emigration," Ph.D. Dissertation, Northwestern University, 1969.

Sibley, James. *Liberia*. New York: Doran and Company, 1928.

Sitterman Carlyle. *Sugar Country: The Sugar Industry in the South, 1753-1950*. Lexington: University of Kentucky Press, 1955.

Slaughter, Philip. *The Virginia History of African Colonization*. Richmond: Macfarlane and Ferguson, 1835.

Smith, Woodruff D. *The German Colonial Empire*. Chapel Hill: University of North Carolina Press, 1978.

Stampp, Kenneth M. *The Peculiar Institution: Slavery in the Ante-Bellum South*. New York: Vintage Books, 1956.

______. *The Era of Reconstruction, 1865-1877*. New York: Vintage Books, 1965.

Starobin, Robert S. *Industrial Slavery in the Old South*. New York: Oxford University press, 1970.

Starr, Frederick. *Liberia: Description, History, and Problems*. Chicago: University of Chicago Press, 1923.

Staudenraus, Philip. *The African Colonization Movement, 1816-1865*. New York: Columbia University Press, 1961.

Stavrianos, L. S. *Global Rift: The Third World Comes of Age*. New York: William Morrow and Company, 1981.

Sundiata, I. K. *Black Scandal: America and the Liberian Labor Crisis, 1919-1936*. Philadelphia: Institute for the Study of Human Issues, 1980.

______. "Prelude to Scandal; Liberia and Fernando Po, 1880- 1930," *Journal of African History*, XV (1974).

Sweezy, Paul M. *Theory of Capitalist Development: Principles of Marxian Political Economy*. New York: Monthly Review Press, 1942.

Sweet, Leonard I. *Black Images of America, 1784-1870*. New York: Norton and Company, 1976.

Syfert, Dwight N. "A Survey of the Liberian Costing Trade, 1822- 1900," *Journal of African History*, XVIII (1977).

Thomas, N. W. "Who Were the Manes?" *Journal of the African Society*, XIX (1919).

Wadstrom, B. C. *Observation on the Slave Trade*. London: Hakluyt Society, 1823.

Washington, H. A. *The Writings of Thomas Jefferson*. Vol. VIII. Washington: Putnam's Sons, 1854.

Wauwermans, H. *Liberia*. Bruxelles: Institute National De Geographie, 1885.

Webster, J. B. and Boahen, A. A. *The Revolutionary Years: West Africa Since 1800*. London: Longmans, 1980.

Welmers, William. "The Mande Languages," *Georgetown University Monographs*, Series No. XI (1958).

West, Richard. *Back to Africa: A History of Sierra Leone and Liberia*. New York: Holt, Rinehart and Winston, Inc., 1970.

Wesley, Charles. "Lincoln's Plan for Colonizing the Emancipated Negroes," *Journal of Negro History*, IV (1919).

Wickstron, Werner. "The American Colonization Society and Liberia: An Historical Study in Religious Motivation and Achievement," Ph.D. Dissertation, Hartford Seminary, 1949.

William, Peter. *A Discourse, Delivered on the Death of Captain Paul Cuffe, before the New York African Institution in the African Methodist Episcopal Zion Church, October 21, 1817*. New York: 1817.

Wilkeson, S. *A Concise History of the Commencement, Progress, and Present Condition of The American Colonies in Liberia*. Washington: Madisonian Office, 1839.

Williams, Eric. *Capitalism and Slavery*. Chapel Hill: University of North Carolina Press, 1944.

Wilson, John. *Western Africa: Its History, Conditions, and Prospects*. New York: Harper and Brothers, 1856.

Wilson, J. W. *Sketches of the Higher Classes of Colored Society in Philadelphia*. Philadelphia: 1841.

Woodward, C. Vann, ed. George Fitzhugh. *Cannibals All!* or *Slaves with Masters*. Cambridge: Harvard University Press, 1973.

Yancy, Ernest Jerome. *Historical Lights of Liberia's Yesterday and Today*. Xenia: The Aldire Publishing Company, 1934.

Young, James C. *Liberia Rediscovered*. New York: Doubleday, Doran and Company, 1936.

INDEX

ABOUT THE AUTHOR

Amos J. Beyan earned his Bachelor of Science degree at Cuttington University College in his native land, Liberia, West Africa, and his Master of Arts at Syracuse University. He is an Assistant Professor of History at Youngstown State University. He has also taught at the State University of New York at Plattsburgh, and at West Virginia University where he earned his Ph.D. in 1985.

His articles have appeared in the *Liberian Studies Journal* and *Journal of Third World Studies*.